The Birth of Jesus
According to the Gospels

The Birth of Jesus
According to the Gospels

Joseph F. Kelly

LITURGICAL PRESS
Collegeville, Minnesota

www.litpress.org

Nihil Obstat: Rev. Robert C. Harren, J.C.L., *Censor deputatus.*
Imprimatur: ✠ Most Rev. John F. Kinney, J.C.D., D.D., Bishop of
St. Cloud, Minnesota, December 31, 2007.

Cover design by David Manahan, OSB. Illustration of the nativity by
the Master of Aviá, Museum of Catalonia.

1   2   3   4   5   6   7   8   9

Library of Congress Cataloging-in-Publication Data

Kelly, Joseph F. (Joseph Francis), 1945–
    The birth of Jesus according to the Gospels / Joseph F. Kelly.
      p. cm.
    Includes bibliographical references.
    ISBN 978-0-8146-2948-2
    1. Jesus Christ—Biography—Sources, Biblical.   I. Title.

BT299.3.K45 2008
232.92—dc22   2007048367

To László Törzsök Jr.,
a good friend and
a good man

Contents

Preface

The Scriptures lie at the heart of Christianity. Our faith in Jesus derives from what the gospels tell us about him and from the witness of the earliest Christians to him. Without the Scriptures, Jesus is simply unknown to us.

This brief book focuses on a very limited area of the Scriptures—a total of four chapters from all of the New Testament, two each from two gospels (Matt 1–2; Luke 1–2). But those four valuable chapters contain the only accounts of Jesus' birth, and scholars call them the infancy narratives. Thanks to the feast of Christmas, they are the most widely known of all New Testament passages, yet they can present problems for believers, even those who do not actually read the gospels. During Advent or the Christmas season a regular churchgoer might one day hear a gospel reading about how the angel Gabriel appeared to Mary who lived in Nazareth of Galilee, and then on another day hear a reading about how Joseph and Mary decided not to return from Egypt to their home in Judea but instead went to Nazareth of Galilee. The attentive churchgoer might wonder if Joseph and Mary lived in Galilee at the time of the annunciation or if they settled there after their return from Egypt. Even more, this churchgoer would legitimately question why the Bible contains apparently contradictory accounts. It is my hope that this book will help the interested reader to understand the gospel accounts of Jesus' birth and to answer questions like this.

In this project I have utilized the most recent findings of biblical scholars and have tried to present them in an accessible way. Furthermore, much of what is in the book derives from my classes and from the questions that my students ask; I suspect that many of their questions may be similar to yours. But let me first answer one question that was asked of me, partly in jest and partly in concern: Will knowing about the infancy narratives somehow "spoil" Christmas? After all, professors often have a well-earned reputation for spoiling people's traditional views, especially about religion. My answer can only be that a better, more thorough knowledge of the Scriptures cannot harm anyone's faith, but rather it can only strengthen that faith. Maybe reading this book might change a little how you have viewed the birth of Jesus, but more accurate understanding of the Nativity will not "spoil" Christmas. After all, even professors celebrate Christmas.

The book's focus falls upon historical and theological questions, but a brief pastoral reflection follows each gospel passage in chapters 3 and 4. I hardly claim expertise in that area, but I hope some readers may find these thoughts helpful.

My thanks to Peter Dwyer and Hans Christoffersen, respectively publisher and editorial director of Liturgical Press, for their interest, support, and assistance. My thanks to Drs. Linda Eisenmann, dean of the College of Arts and Sciences at John Carroll University, and David LaGuardia, academic vice-president, for granting me a reduced load for research which enabled me to write this book. My thanks to Dr. Mary Beadle, former dean of the graduate school and director of research, and to the members of the JCU University Committee on Research and Service for a 2006 summer fellowship and funds that allowed me to do the research for this book and to purchase titles in the field. My thanks to my friend and department colleague, Dr. Sheila McGinn, from whom I have learned a great deal about the New Testament. My thanks also to my former graduate assistants, Alicia Lee and Devon

Lynch-Huggins, for their assistance in reading the manu-
script. Very special thanks go to Mrs. Gina Messina-Dysert,
whose graduate thesis on the infancy narratives and the Old
Testament helped me better to understand the relationship
between the two, and some of whose insights appear in the
text. Further special thanks to our department secretary,
Kathryn Merhar, whose remarkable efficiency allowed an
overworked and underappreciated department chairperson (as
I usually think of myself) to have some spare time to work on
this book. Any deficiencies in the book are solely my
responsibility.

As always, my sincerest thanks go to my wife Ellen, a
thoughtful and generous spouse, who took time from her own
busy schedule to make myriad sacrifices, both large and
small, so that I would have the time to write.

This book is dedicated to László Törzsök Jr., a good friend
to my wife and me for three decades.

Joseph F. Kelly
Feast of Saint Nicholas, 2007

Some helps to following the text:

> This book will cite the Bible frequently, so here is an explanation of the citations:
>
> Mark 4:1-12 means the Gospel of Mark, chapter 4, verses 1 to 12.

You need not have a Bible with you to read the book, but you may want to look up a passage or two. For example, the book will often cite a verse without quoting it, such as Micah 5:2, which refers to a prophecy by the Israelite prophet Micah, which the gospel writer Matthew says that Jesus' birth fulfilled. You may want to look up the passage in Micah on your own. Also, this book gives the text of the infancy narratives in pieces as part of the discussion, but it may be helpful to first read through each of the narratives straight through (Matt 1–2 and Luke 1–2) in the Bible before getting deeper into the discussion in this book.

The New Testament books will be cited most frequently, so here is a list of them:

Gospels: Matthew, Mark, Luke, John

Epistles: Romans, 1 and 2 Corinthians, Galatians, Philemon, Philippians, 1 Thessalonians *(these are epistles written by Paul)*; 2 Thessalonians, Ephesians, Colossians, Hebrews, 1 and 2 Timothy, Titus *(these are epistles attributed to Paul but not actually written by him)*; James, Jude, 1, 2, and 3 John, 1 and 2 Peter

Theological history of first community: Acts of the Apostles (cited simply as Acts)

Visionary book: Revelation (also called the Apocalypse)

CHAPTER ONE

The Gospels and History

Surprisingly for many Christians, the birth of Jesus appears in just two places in the New Testament (NT), the first two chapters of Matthew's gospel and the first two chapters of Luke's gospel. Although pagan and Jewish sources can fill in some background, what we directly know of the Nativity depends upon what those gospels tell us. So naturally we have to ask, what exactly do the gospel accounts say? It sounds like a straightforward question, but nothing is straightforward in modern biblical studies.

Unfortunately, for centuries the gospels have been understood as "lives" or biographies of Jesus, and many contemporary Christians still use those terms. But even a quick reading shows that this cannot be so. Only two gospels give an account of his birth, and neither of them gives the day or the year. Only one, Luke (2:41-50), mentions anything about Jesus between his birth and his public career. All four gospels focus on Jesus' ministry in Galilee and then his brief but fateful journey to Jerusalem and death, but no gospel gives the exact date of his death. Clearly these are not biographies as modern people understand the term. Can you imagine reading a biography of Jane Austen or Abraham Lincoln that provided no dates and started when the subject was already almost thirty years old (Luke 3:23)?

Furthermore, when we compare the gospel narratives about Jesus' public career, we find that they do not always agree with one another. For example, Matthew, Mark, and Luke tell us that Jesus drove the money-changers from the temple at the end of his ministry, whereas John puts that episode at the beginning. Matthew 6:9-13 and Luke 11:2-4 have different versions of the Lord's Prayer (Matthew's is the familiar one). Clearly, "lives" of Jesus that do not agree with one another on the basic facts or words cannot be biographies as we think of them today.

Does this mean that we have no reliable information about Jesus' life? Absolutely not. But it does mean that we must understand what the gospels actually are.

Rather than biographies, they are theological accounts of Jesus' public career. The *evangelists* (gospel writers) wrote as believing Christians for other believing Christians, not as secular historians writing for a general audience. To use a technical term, each evangelist produced a *Christology*, that is, a theology of Christ.

When a theologian writes a Christology, she or he tries to show that the mystery of Christ, comprehensible only by faith, can be truly if incompletely understood by the believer. The evangelists passed along their faith in Jesus as the Son of God, the redeemer of the world, the Messiah, the first-born of the new creation, and the founder and foundation of the Christian faith. Following the path laid down by the Apostle Paul in his letters, the evangelists ultimately wrote about the Risen Christ because if Christ were not risen, the Christians' faith was in vain (1 Cor 15:14). The resurrection vindicated all that Jesus said and did.

But in order for their readers to understand the risen Christ who continues to work for the salvation of believers, the evangelists had to give some account of Jesus' earthly life, since his whole life led up to his resurrection. We want to determine what biographical information the evangelists provide about his birth and how they incorporated the infancy narratives into their gospels.

To answer those questions, we must start with how the gospels came to be. Jesus himself did not write anything, and his words and deeds were passed along orally for decades before being written down by his followers. In an era when we can record things on DVDs, CDs, the internet, digital cameras, hard drives, and even paper, it is difficult for us to understand oral tradition, but for the ancient world that was the norm. To use the second-most-famous ancient example, we have no writings from the great Greek philosopher Socrates (469–399 BC) but only accounts passed on primarily by his disciple, another great Greek philosopher, Plato (427–347 BC).

Yet even if we acknowledge that oral tradition was the ancient practice, we still have to worry that some event would slip out of its historical or chronological framework or that words could be forgotten or twisted around. That is true, but scholars can only work with what the ancients have left us. In fact, for many ancient people, the *advantage* of oral tradition was that a saying or event could be modified to suit an audience, something even modern Christians do. For example, in the parables, Jesus often uses rural imagery (wheat field, vineyard, sheep, sowing seed) which would be largely unfamiliar to children living in a city. Christians ministering in those areas might change the setting to a familiar urban one in order to make the spiritual point of Jesus' parable more understandable. We will examine examples of such adaptation when we get to the gospels of Matthew and Luke.

Furthermore, ancient people who used oral traditions did not discard historical traditions wholesale, and most attempted to be historically accurate. As we shall soon see, the gospels show strong agreement on many major points in Jesus' life.

Several other characteristics of ancient writing impact our approach to the gospels. Modern historians strive for objectivity, but ancient writers did not. Instead, most wrote to push a political or patriotic point, such as showing the greatness of their peoples: the Greeks demonstrated their superiority to the Persian "barbarians," the Romans claimed that their empire fulfilled their destiny, and the Jews made the claim—so absurd to the Greeks and Romans!—that the one God had chosen them among all the nations of the world to be his special people. When the evangelists wrote to proclaim their faith in Jesus rather than give an objective biography of him, they were writing like typical ancient historians.

We must understand even more about ancient historians: they were allowed to put speeches in the mouths of their characters in order to move the narrative along, something which would destroy the reputation of a modern historian. For example, the Roman historian Tacitus (AD 57–117) recorded the empire's conquest of Britain, and he recounts a brilliant speech by a British tribal leader who urged his soldiers to resist Roman tyranny. But Tacitus never went to Britain and knew not a word of the British language. He simply created a Latin speech that a British tribal leader *should* have given in those circumstances. This approach partly explains why we sometimes find different versions of Jesus' words in different gospels, and it will also explain some significant passages in Luke's infancy narrative.

Finally, we must also recall that the evangelists wrote decades after Jesus' death and outside of Palestine. Scholars date the gospel of Mark around the year 70, those of Matthew and Luke to the 80s, and John's gospel around 100. By the time they wrote, Christianity had expanded from its Near Eastern home into the wider Roman, Mediterranean world, and especially into the Jewish *Diaspora* or Dispersion, that is, the residence of Jews outside the historical land of Israel, which the Romans called Judea. Although the Diaspora started with the Babylonian Exile of the sixth century BC, it changed significantly two centuries later when the conquests of Alexander the Great brought Greek culture and language to the Near East. Many Diasporan Jews lived in Greek-speaking territories, such as Egypt and Syria, and in Mediterranean cities such as Alexandria and Antioch.

The first Christian writer, the Apostle Paul, was a Diasporan Jew from Roman Asia Minor (modern Turkey) who brought Christianity into the world outside Judea, a world of Diasporan Jews and Gentile pagans. So when Paul, the evangelists, and all other NT authors composed their works, they wrote in Greek, the language of their intended readers. That sounds obvious, but it has a consequence. Jesus spoke a language called Aramaic, a Semitic dialect widely used in the Near East. Some Aramaic words (*talitha cum* and *ephphatha* in Mark 5:41 and 7:34) appear in the gospels, but otherwise Jesus' words are recorded *in Greek*, which means that the words of Jesus survive in a translation. Knowing this Greek background will help us to understand passages in the infancy narratives.

In recent years many believers have heard in the media about non-biblical books, such as the *Gospel of Judas*, which supposedly have biographical information about Jesus. These books form what scholars call the Apocryphal New Testament, that is, books which claim to be by or about NT figures but which were not accepted into the Bible by the early Christians. These books, mostly written in the second and third centuries, tell us a lot about the Christians who produced them and about their religious views, such as a significant interest in Jesus' birth, but no scholar considers them to be reliable historical sources, especially for biographical information about Jesus.

Clearly a huge gap exists between ourselves and the ancients on what constitutes history. Let me close this section by citing advice the Irish biblical scholar Wilfrid Harrington, OP, received early in his career: "When someone in our western culture hears a story, the spontaneous reaction is: 'Is it true?' When an ancient Semite heard a story, the spontaneous question was: 'What does it mean?' . . . We want the infancy narratives of Matthew and Luke to be wholly historical. What we have to face is the fact that neither is conventionally historical—nor was ever intended to be" (for information on Harrington's book, see "Suggested Reading").

When we acknowledge the gospels to be products of the ancient world, we can understand why they cannot be modern biographies. But do the gospels provide any reliable biographical information? Actually, they provide quite a bit, not in the sense that we can say that Jesus told a particular parable on March 10 in AD 31, but in the sense of a general chronological outline, some historical information, and insights into Jesus' character.

Here are some points which one or more of the gospels provide that we can consider biographical:

- Jesus' parents were named Mary (Miriam) and Joseph.
- Joseph was a carpenter.
- Jesus followed his father's profession, normal for a boy of that era.
- He was born in Bethlehem in Judea during the reign of Herod.
- He grew up in Nazareth in Galilee.
- His parents were pious Jews.
- He received a good education in his faith since at age twelve he could impress temple scholars with his knowledge.
- He had brothers and sisters (although many Christians believe them to have been cousins or some other relatives).
- He could read, unusual but not unheard of for a carpenter.
- The public ministry of John the Baptist preceded his own.
- Some of John's disciples left him and followed Jesus.
- He had disciples of both sexes who followed him.
- He chose twelve male disciples for special roles.
- His ministry was spent almost completely in Galilee.
- He was a popular preacher and wonder worker.
- He was a kind man, willing to help those on the margins of society.
- He spoke the truth, regardless of the price he had to pay.

- He had the common touch, able to relate to people of all classes, from aristocrats to beggars.
- He never discriminated against women but gave them the respect that ancient culture denied them.
- He saw past ethnic differences, seeing the good in Samaritans, Romans, and other non-Jews.
- He showed great respect for the Jewish Law.
- Although he believed in his mission, he observed the Jewish Law.
- He had conflicts with a religious group called the Pharisees.
- His debates with the Pharisees were often not about the Law but about the Pharisees' understanding of it.
- He could show respect for Roman law because God's law transcended mere human law, for example, the tribute money with Caesar's image.
- He was careful not to let people believe he had political goals and always stressed his ministry was religious.
- Even though he was a layperson and not a formal religious scholar, he could debate as an equal with priests, religious lawyers, and scholars.
- He had great insight into human nature and could see both the positives and negatives in people, such as the rich young man who truly wanted to follow him but could not abandon his wealth.
- He traveled constantly with his disciples, even into non-Jewish territories.
- He had a sense of his calling and the courage to fulfill it.
- After a ministry in Galilee, he went to Jerusalem, where some of the local authorities banded together against him.
- His enemies engineered his condemnation by the Roman governor, Pontius Pilate.
- He was crucified.
- He rose from the dead.

This list of items could be extended, but it demonstrates that even if the gospels are not modern biographies, they still provide much general biographical information about Jesus. With this in mind, we can turn to the infancy narratives as long as we remember one more point that relates especially to them.

When we read the infancy narratives, we do it through a wonderful prism, Christmas. The words "A decree went forth from Caesar Augustus that the whole world should be enrolled . . ." will always have us thinking of lights, trees, decorations, a crèche, and so much more. But there was no Christmas in the first century. To be sure, we often call the infancy narratives the first Christmas, but Christmas, *the feast that honors Jesus' birth*, did not come into existence until the third century and maybe not until the fourth, while "Christmas," an Anglo-Saxon word, did not appear until the eleventh century. This is why scholars refer to the gospel accounts of Jesus' birth as the Nativity rather than the first Christmas. This in turn means that Matthew and Luke did not write their infancy narratives for a then non-existent feast but rather as the opening chapters of their gospels, and that is how the infancy narratives must be understood. We may not have to read the entire gospels of Matthew and Luke to understand the infancy narratives, but we should always bear in mind that the opening chapters are leading the reader toward Jesus' public life and ministry.

CHAPTER TWO

Matthew, Luke, and Their Gospels

Matthew and Luke

Since only the gospels of Matthew and Luke tell us of Jesus' birth, let us consider what we know about these two evangelists.

Matthew

Matthew was a Galilean tax collector, called by Jesus to be one of the Twelve Apostles (Matt 9:9), right? Actually, no. Many misimpressions about the gospels have been around for centuries, and most books on Scripture have to begin by correcting those impressions—sometimes to the disappointment of readers—but scholarship can only help our understanding of the Bible.

The first gospel has had Matthew's name attached to it since the second century, but there is no name on the gospel itself, nor does this identification of Matthew as the evangelist appear anywhere else in the New Testament. If Matthew were a Galilean tax collector, he would have been a native Aramaic speaker and probably would have written his gospel in that language. But like all NT literature, Matthew's gospel survives in Greek. If the evangelist originally wrote it in a Semitic tongue, we would expect the Greek version to show the marks of a translation, such as stilted phraseology or jumbled sentence structure, yet we find none of that. The author could have been a native Aramaic speaker who wrote in Greek, but then we would expect some evidence that Greek was not his first language, such as the occasional awkward phrase, but the evangelist wrote Greek fluently and easily. Clearly Greek was his native language, suggesting he was by birth a Diasporan rather than a Palestinian Jew.

Even stronger evidence survives that the evangelist was not one of the twelve apostles. Since the nineteenth century, scholars have recognized that the gospels of Matthew, Mark, and Luke are related. One scholar suggested the relationship was so strong that one could look at them all with one eye, giving rise to the term "Synoptic" or "with the eye" gospels. If you put these three gospels in three parallel columns, you can go through the columns and see how much material the gospels share. Clearly the evangelists were drawing from similar sources, but biblical scholars believe that one gospel was the major source for the other two. But which one?

On the surface, we have an easy answer. Matthew, one of the Twelve, wrote first, and Mark and Luke, who did not know Jesus during his lifetime, naturally depended upon Matthew the eyewitness. But this simple explanation has a major flaw, and that is the Gospel of Mark. Christian tradition since the second century identified the author of the second gospel as Mark, sometimes called John Mark, one of Paul's disciples (Acts 12:12, 25; 15:37, 39; Phlm 24). While modern scholars generally deny that this Mark wrote the gospel, the important point here is that its author was not one of the Twelve as Matthew supposedly was.

Mark is the shortest gospel and has the smallest amount of unique material. Fully 91 percent of what is in Mark appears in either Matthew or Luke, while much of what is in the other two does not appear in Mark. To focus just on Matthew and Mark, if Matthew wrote first, and if Mark read his gospel and then abbreviated what he took from it, we must wonder why Mark would have left out so much. Not only does his gospel have no infancy narrative, it also lacks the Lord's

Prayer, the eight beatitudes, major parables, and Jesus' post-resurrection appearances. Omission of one or two of these might make some sense, but all of them?

When Mark does include material that Matthew has, more problems emerge. For example, Mark says simply that Satan tempted Jesus (1:13), whereas Matthew describes the scene more fully, including a dialogue between Jesus and Satan (4:1-11). Why would Mark leave that out? It simply defies credulity that Mark would have had Matthew's gospel in front of him when he wrote and discarded all of this remarkable material.

Mark's style also presents problems if he borrowed from Matthew. To put it charitably, Mark writes clumsily at times. Many examples survive, but one story demonstrates it best.

> On that day, when evening had come, he [Jesus] said to them, "Let us go across to the other side [of the lake]." And leaving the crowd behind, they took him with them in the boat, just as he was. *Other boats* were with him. A great windstorm arose, and the waves beat into the boat, so that the boat was already being swamped. But he was in the stern, asleep on the cushion; and *they woke him up* and said to him, "Teacher, do you not care that we are perishing?" *He woke up* and rebuked the wind, and said to the sea, "Peace! Be still!" Then the wind ceased, and there was a dead calm. (Mark 4:35-39, emphasis added)

Notice that Mark never tells us what happened to the other boats, a significant omission given the severity of the storm. Far more problematically, Jesus wakes up *twice*, the second time occurring when the disciples had already been talking to him!

Matthew recounts the same event (8:23-27), but he makes no mention of other boats, and Jesus wakes up only once, a far more logical and sensible account. We must ask, what makes more sense: that Mark took Matthew's account and added confusing and even contradictory details or that Matthew took Mark's account and deleted the confusing details? And to this example, many others could be added.

But if Matthew used Mark's gospel, the crucial issue arises: if Matthew were indeed one of the twelve apostles, why would he, an eyewitness to Jesus' public ministry, rely upon an account written by someone who was not?

The good quality of Matthew's Greek, the additional material, the sharper writing, all point in the same direction. Matthew used Mark as a basis for his gospel. The author of the first gospel and the Matthew of the twelve apostles were different persons.

So who then was the author of the first gospel? To begin with, we cannot be sure if his name was Matthew since that comes from a second-century source which identified him with the Galilean tax collector. But since we have no other name, scholars use the familiar one to refer to the evangelist.

All the evidence about him comes from the gospel itself. First, he was a native Greek speaker and thus not likely to have grown up in Galilee. Second, he knew Jewish customs well, and, as we shall see in some detail, he put much emphasis on connections between Jesus and the Hebrew Bible (the Christian Old Testament), so he most likely converted to Christianity from Judaism and was thus a Diasporan Jew from the Eastern Mediterranean. He probably wrote his gospel in that area, although he surely had visited Palestine.

When the Acts of the Apostles recounts Paul's life, it tells of opposition and even conflict between Christians and Jews. Matthew's gospel (28:11-15) indicates that his community also had poor relations with the local Jewish community, which explains some of his defensiveness about Jesus' Judaism, as we shall see.

He may well have been a civil servant of some kind, and possibly even a tax collector, since he could write in an age when few people did. His gospel also contains sophisticated theology, which indicates more than a basic education.

Beyond this little bit, we cannot say more about the author of the first gospel. But this sparse information does not weaken the gospel's value. The key point is that the early

Christians accepted this as an inspired book, worthy of inclusion in the biblical canon.

Luke

What about the author of the third gospel? Like that of Matthew, this gospel has no name attached. Second-century Christian tradition attributes it to Luke, a "fellow worker" of Paul (Phlm 24), who reappears in 2 Timothy (4:11) and who is called "the beloved physician" in Colossians 4:14, two letters attributed to Paul but not actually written by him. The identification of the evangelist with the NT Luke is debated, and so scholars hesitate to identify the two, although, as with Matthew, they use the familiar name. But we do know one very sure thing about Luke besides what this gospel tells us, and that is essential for understanding the gospel: he wrote the Acts of the Apostles, thus being the only evangelist to write a second book. The first half of Acts recounts the story of the Jerusalem church immediately after the resurrection, while the second half focuses on Luke's hero, the apostle Paul. Scholars often rely upon Acts to interpret passages in the gospel and vice versa. Many scholars refer to the two books together as Luke-Acts, an indication of their fundamental unity.

These two books strongly suggest that Luke was a Gentile. He knows the Gentile world very well, whereas he makes some mistakes about Jewish geography and customs, as we shall see. He knows how the Roman Empire functions. In his books governors and proconsuls and centurions are all exactly where they should be, as are local municipal officials. Scholars cannot pinpoint where he wrote his gospel—possibly Syria (Antioch) or Greece or even Rome—but they date the gospel to the 80s of the first century, that is, contemporaneous with Matthew, although, as the infancy narratives demonstrate, they did not know one another's works.

Luke had a superb education because he is the New Testament's best stylist. Everyone from rich to poor speaks well in his books, even at the cost of historical accuracy. For example, illiterate peasants and Roman governors sound more or less alike. The verbal class distinctions of *My Fair Lady* do not exist in this gospel. Also, no evangelist could tell a story like Luke. The proof is simple: his parables are the ones we remember most easily—the Prodigal Son, the Pharisee and Publican (also referred to as the Tax Collector), the Rich Man and Lazarus, and the Good Samaritan. Like Matthew, he was also a good theologian.

Was the author of the third gospel the physician so familiar in Christian tradition? He does use medical terminology occasionally, but he uses terms familiar to most educated people, much the way modern people with no medical training speak of germs and viruses. On the other hand, if the terms were so familiar, why is he the only NT writer to use them? And did the Luke who is mentioned in the NT books even write this gospel? The questions remain unanswered, and they really do not impact our understanding of the book. As with Matthew, the book's importance lies in its acceptance as inspired and canonical by the early church.

The Gospels of Matthew and Luke

Before turning to the two gospels, we should deal with the widespread notions that the evangelists wrote their gospels to prove to Jews and pagans that Jesus was the true Messiah sent by God, and that the evangelists achieved this by recounting Jesus' miracles. Not so on either count. Let us take the second point first.

In the gospels themselves, Jesus does not perform miracles so that people will believe in him. Repeatedly Jesus expects faith *before* performing a miracle. He tells the Canaanite woman whose daughter he heals, "Woman, great is your faith" (Matt 15:28). He tells Jairus and his wife to have faith, and their daughter will be healed (Luke 8:50). He assures the blind man, "your faith has saved you" (Luke 18:42). Sometimes the faith is not of an individual but of a group, as in the cure of the paralytic. "When Jesus saw *their* faith [the friends who carried the paralytic on a pallet] . . ." (Mark 2:5).

The evangelists followed their Lord; they did not use miracles to engender faith but presumed that their readers had it already. So when we look at the infancy narratives, we must recall that the miraculous elements (the star, the angels appearing to the shepherds) are not there to win over pagans or Jews, but because they were genuine traditions about Jesus' birth known to Matthew and Luke and most likely to the communities for which they wrote.

This leads us to the first point: like all biblical authors, the evangelists wrote as believing Christians for other believing Christians, as members of early Christian communities for other members of those communities. The evangelists do not try to prove Jesus is the Son of God, the Son of Man, the Messiah, or anything else. Mark's gospel begins directly: "The beginning of the good news of Jesus Christ, the Son of God" (1:1). Mark just states it, and that is that. The other evangelists followed Mark's lead, and they got this approach from the familiar source of so many early Christian practices, the Jews.

Look how the ancient Israelites began the Old Testament: "In the beginning when God created the heavens and the earth. . ." (Gen 1:1). Notice there is no attempt to prove that God exists but just a description of his creative work, because the author was a believing Israelite writing for other believing Israelites. The book of Isaiah opens with a direct assertion: "The vision of Isaiah son of Amoz, which he saw concerning Judah and Jerusalem." No skepticism about the authenticity of the vision, but rather a simple acceptance that God spoke to and through the great prophet. All the biblical books are books of faith, and the same can be said of the sacred books of other world religions.

Now that we understand that Matthew and Luke wrote for their fellow believers, we must ask why they added infancy narratives to the basic account provided by Mark. As we saw, they were not writing accounts of Jesus' birth for a feast day, but rather they were writing the introductory chapters of their gospels. That means that somewhere between the writing of Mark's gospel about the year 70 and the writing of their own gospels in the 80s, Matthew and Luke saw the need to add to Mark's gospel narrative an account of Jesus' birth. What was that need?

The need was a basic one: Christology. Matthew and Luke felt uncomfortable with Mark's portrayal of Jesus, and especially with how he showed Jesus achieving recognition of his divine sonship. The first event in Jesus' life narrated by Mark is his baptism by John the Baptist. "And just as he [Jesus] was coming up out of the water, he saw the heavens torn apart and the Spirit descending like a dove on him. And a voice came from heaven, 'You are my Son, the Beloved; with you I am well pleased'" (Mark 1:10-11).

To modern Christians, who know all four gospels and who consider John the Baptist as a forerunner of Jesus, this passage presents no problems. But look at it in mid-first century terms when Mark's was still the *only* written gospel. Mark says that God recognized Jesus as his son *after* his baptism. First-century Christians might understandably wonder if God had recognized him before that. More problematically, these Christians may have wondered if there were a causal relationship between the baptism and the recognition. If so, that would make John the Baptist a major factor, perhaps *the* major factor, in Jesus' receiving divine recognition. Scholars do not believe that this is what Mark meant, but we can see how such confusion could have arisen.

But there is more. Everyone "knows" that John played the role of forerunner to Jesus, and he decreased as Jesus increased (John 3:30). Not exactly. The Acts of the Apostles tells us that in the mid-50s, two of the apostle Paul's coworkers in Ephesus, Priscilla and Aquila, met a Jew named Apollos, who came from Alexandria in Egypt and who "knew only the baptism of John" (Acts 18:25). When Paul himself was in Ephesus, he met a dozen disciples who knew nothing about the Holy Spirit but had received the baptism of John (Acts 19:1-7). Although we cannot say for sure if these were disciples of Christ or John, the key point is that John's movement did not die with him. Christians encountered people who had been baptized by his disciples and maybe even were his disciples, and they encountered them twenty-five years after John's death and hundreds of miles from Palestine. At the very least John's life and teaching continued to move people for some time after his death. On some occasions and in some places the movements might have rivaled each other.

A non-biblical support for a possible rivalry can be found in a third-century work entitled *The Pseudo-Clementine Recognitions*, written in Greek, definitely from the Eastern Mediterranean, and possibly containing material that dates to the first century. The book claims to be the work of Clement of Rome, a Christian writer of the end of the first century and, in Roman Catholic tradition, the third successor of Peter the apostle as bishop of Rome. Many pseudepigraphic (falsely named) texts are attributed to him. In the *Recognitions*, one of John the Baptist's disciples tells Jesus' disciples that "[John] is the Christ and not Jesus, just as Jesus himself said concerning him. . . ." A tradition of John's superiority to Jesus, although not widespread, survived in the Eastern Mediterranean for at least two centuries.

Now the concern of Matthew and Luke makes sense. They did not wish believers to think that Jesus owed his recognition as God's son to his baptism by John. They had to demonstrate that he had such recognition long before his baptism, and so, collecting traditions about Jesus' nativity, they demonstrated that he received divine recognition at his very birth. Indeed, the annunciation stories showed he received the recognition even before his birth. Thanks to Matthew and Luke, Jesus' story begins not with his baptism but with his birth, which these two evangelists added to Mark's basic narrative.

But they added a great deal more than just the infancy narratives. Reworking Mark's material and adding to it, Matthew and Luke created their own Christologies, ones suitable for their own communities.

This can raise concerns among modern believers. How could the evangelists have created their own Christologies? Jesus was one person, not four. Would not four Christologies distort our understanding of him?

Rare for biblical scholarship, this problem has a simple answer. Think of who you are. You are one person to your family members, another to your coworkers or fellow students, another to your neighbors, yet another to people in clubs or on teams, and, if you have joined an internet chat group, you present still another picture to people who have not even met you. You are a different person to different people, yet you are one and the same.

The New Testament refers to Jesus as the Messiah, the Savior, the Lamb of God, the Son of Man, the vine, the eternal high priest, the fulfillment of prophecies, the Word, the Good Shepherd, the way, the truth, and the life, and the Alpha and Omega—and this is just a partial list. Nor is such an approach to Jesus just a literary one. He was ethnically Jewish, but medieval and renaissance artists portrayed him as a European. Today Third World Christians portray him as an African, a Latin American, or an Asian, and not just visually. Yet all these portrayals are of one and the same person.

So why are there so many different portrayals? Because all Christians believe that Jesus has relevance for them, and they want to express that. The New Testament authors shared this view. They wrote for diverse audiences, stressing particular aspects of Jesus' person and mission, but they never equated those aspects with the totality of his person and mission. The unknown author of the Epistle to the Hebrews is the only NT writer who calls Jesus a high priest, clearly an issue of importance to Jewish converts who grew up with devotion to the temple and who were prominent among the epistle's readers.

But the author of Hebrews does not claim that "high priest" is the sole way to understand Jesus. Rather, this is the understanding of Jesus which he wishes to develop for his readers. Matthew and Luke would do the same for their readers.

Matthew's Gospel

We already know that Matthew wrote for a Greek-speaking audience, most likely a combined community of both Gentiles and Diasporan Jews. Strikingly, Matthew ends his gospel with the risen Christ's words to his disciples, "Go therefore and make disciples of all nations, baptizing them in the name of the Father and of the Son and of the Holy Spirit" (28:19). This famous verse makes it clear that the Christian message must go to all peoples, the vast majority of whom would have been Gentiles. The passage says clearly what appears in more subtle ways throughout the gospel, for example, at Jesus' death. "Now when the centurion and those with him [under the cross], who were keeping watch over Jesus, saw the earthquake and what took place, they were terrified and said, 'Truly this man was God's Son'" (27:54). Gentiles, the very Romans who executed Jesus, recognized who he was, while the Jewish leaders refused to do so. Matthew leaves no doubt that this growing religious movement has its future in Gentile lands.

But this gospel also pays more attention to Judaism than any other gospel. Matthew cites the Old Testament (OT) twice as often as any other evangelist, and he cites more different passages from the OT than any other evangelist. Only Matthew records Jesus' words, "I have come not to abolish [the law] but to fulfill it. For truly I tell you, until heaven and earth pass away, not one letter, not one stroke of a letter, will pass from the law until all is accomplished" (5:17-18). Such a stunning validation of the Mosaic Law from Jesus himself would have immense significance for Jewish converts, who naturally would have wondered about the status of the Law that God had given to their people. Matthew further expressed his reverence for the Law by paralleling Jesus with Moses, the great lawgiver of ancient Israel.

Moses received the Law on Mount Sinai, and in the Sermon on the Mount (Matt 5–7), Jesus gives the new law. Scholars believe that although Jesus no doubt used local high places to teach, the Sermon is largely of Matthew's creation. They think this because if you look at the parallel passages in the gospels, sayings uttered by Jesus in one sermon in Matthew appear in a variety of places in Luke. Does it make more sense that Luke knew about a brilliant sermon but deliberately broke it up or that Matthew took a number of sayings and put them into a larger sermon? Most scholars think the latter, and for good reason—Jewish converts would recognize the Moses/Jesus parallels. Including the Sermon on the Mount, Matthew records five long discourses of Jesus (5:1–7:29; 10:35–11:1; 13:1-52; 18:1-35; 24:1–25:46), and possibly he wanted to parallel these with the five books of the Torah, traditionally attributed to Moses. At the Transfiguration, Jesus' face "shone like the sun" (Matt 17:2), paralleling Exodus 34:30 which recounts that Moses' face shone like the sun when he came down from Mount Sinai.

Many other appeals to Jewish converts appear in the book, often in less obvious ways. For example, although Matthew shows Jesus in spirited debates with the Pharisees, he often shows Jesus giving them respect, something Luke rarely does. Both gospels rework Mark's account (Mark 2:23-28) of how Jesus' disciples picked grain on the Sabbath, a violation of that sacred day, which Jesus justifies by an appeal to a similar act by the great Israelite king David (Matt 12:1-8; Luke 6:1-5). In Luke's gospel, when the Pharisees see what is happening, they say to Jesus, "Why are *you* doing what is wrong on the Sabbath?" They outright accuse Jesus himself. But Matthew, aware of Jewish sensibilities, treats the matter very differently.

For starters, he adds the important detail that the disciples were hungry, so they did not just pick the grain arbitrarily. The Pharisees do not accuse Jesus of violating the Sabbath but instead say to him, "Look, your disciples are doing what is not lawful to do on the Sabbath," thus implying that Jesus may not have known what the disciples were up to. Unlike Luke, who has the Pharisees accuse Jesus, Matthew shows the Pharisees treating Jesus fairly and giving him the benefit of the doubt. When Jesus responds to them, he uses the same Davidic example that Mark and Luke do, but he also does the Pharisees the courtesy of providing a second example. Jesus recognizes them as scholars of the Law, and he wants to justify his disciples' actions.

A final example of Matthew's concern for the sensitivities of Jewish converts is a very subtle one. All three synoptic evangelists recount how a Jerusalem mob, incited by Jesus' enemies, demanded that Pilate release Barabbas and execute Jesus, that is, they chose the evil man over the good one. Mark 15:7 and Luke 23:19 identify Barabbas as a revolutionary, but Matthew says simply that he was "a notorious prisoner" (27:16). Why would Matthew leave out so important a fact as Barabbas' being a revolutionary? Because Jewish readers might consider a rebel against Rome to be a hero, which would frustrate Matthew's central point, that the mob chose the evil man over the good one.

Matthew's Christology gives us a very Jewish Jesus, who indeed comes to save all peoples but who respects Jewish institutions, traditions and groups, who observes the Law, and who fulfills the Old Testament prophecies. For Matthew's Jewish-Christian readers, fulfilling the prophecies proves that Jesus was the Messiah, the Christ, who came not on clouds and power but instead to serve, to suffer, and to die to redeem the human race from its sins. This Jewish Jesus will dominate Matthew's infancy narrative, but never to the exclusion of the Savior's mission to the Gentiles as well.

Luke's Gospel

When we turn not only to the Gospel of Luke but also to the Acts of the Apostles, we find a writer who portrays a Jewish

Jesus and who shows the apostle Paul agonizing over the relation of Christianity to Judaism, but whose overall approach differs considerably from Matthew's because Luke is writing for a mostly Gentile audience. This focus appears in a variety of ways, and here is a small but telling one. All three gospels tell how Jesus cured the paralytic whose friends brought him to Jesus. Recall that the friends cannot get into the building where Jesus is preaching, so they go up on the roof, where Mark (2:4) says they "dug through" the roof, something they could do to a typical Palestinian roof made of sticks and packed earth, which in turn would be something difficult for Greeks and Romans to comprehend. When Luke retells the narrative, he says that they *removed the tiles* (5:19), proving that he wrote for an audience familiar with Greek and Roman houses.

Another good example appears in the story of Jesus and Barabbas. As we saw, Matthew does not mention that Barabbas was a revolutionary, not wanting to make him sympathetic to Jewish readers. In his account, Luke focuses on Pontius Pilate, the Roman governor. Aware that Gentiles would react in anger or disgust at learning that Jesus died a traitor's death and that they would want nothing to do with a religion founded by someone condemned by the imperial government, Luke works overtime to show that Jesus was innocent and died only because of a weak and incompetent Roman governor.

Three times (23:4, 14, 23) Pilate publicly acknowledges Jesus' innocence. While Mark says that Barabbas committed murder during an insurrection, Luke asserts Barabbas was in prison for "insurrection and murder" (23:25), effectively separating the two crimes and implying that Barabbas did not kill someone in the confused melee of an insurrection but was actually both a revolutionary and a murderer. This is the man whom Pilate set free! Nor does Luke actually mention Pilate's order for Jesus' execution; rather "he handed Jesus over as they wished" (23:25), that is, the governor caved in to the mob. Luke emphasizes Pilate's moral weakness and appalling incompetence. So anxious is the evangelist to prove the injustice of Jesus' death that he becomes heavy-handed. Whereas Matthew and Mark show the Roman centurion under the cross acknowledging, "Truly this man was God's son," Luke has the centurion say, "Certainly this man was innocent" (23:47).

Luke makes his point: Greeks and Romans need not worry about this new religion. Far from being a criminal, its founder was a good man who fell victim to a venal, weak, pathetic governor who openly acknowledged the founder's innocence—a far different interpretation of the Jesus-Barabbas account than that which Matthew gave to his Jewish-Christian audience.

Other details appear that would relate to a Gentile audience. Only Luke mentions any of the Caesars by name, Augustus (2:1), Tiberius (3:1), and Claudius (Acts 11:28), so he sets the events of Jesus' life and that of the early church in a Roman context. Luke even tells how the Apostle Paul debated with "some Epicurean and Stoic philosophers" (Acts 17:18), showing the new revelation encountering the wisdom of the classical world. As noted earlier, Luke places Roman officials exactly where they are supposed to be, and he does not need to identify their functions for his readers.

So what Christology does Luke offer his Gentile audience? He emphasizes Jesus as the universal savior. For example, only in Luke do we find the parable of the Good Samaritan, that is, a non-Jew and a member of a people whom most Jews loathed (10:29-37). Jesus tells it in response to a question from a religious lawyer, "Who is my neighbor?" When he asks the lawyer which of the three men in the story was the neighbor of the robbers' victim, the lawyer responds, "The one who showed him mercy." He cannot even bring himself to mention the word "Samaritan," yet this Samaritan is the one whom Jesus chose as a model of charity. This universalism appears repeatedly in the Acts of the Apostles, where Roman officials repeatedly save Paul's life from angry pagan and Jewish mobs (Acts 19:28-41; 21:30–22:29).

But Luke extended his universality beyond geographic lines to include social ones. Because Jewish tax collectors worked for the Romans and had to handle coins with the images of emperors and even pagan deities, which was an impious act, most Jews had contempt for them. Yet in the parable of the Pharisee and the tax collector (traditionally called the publican), Jesus asserts that the humble tax collector, who admits he is a sinner, "went down to his home justified" while the self-righteous Pharisee, who measured his sanctity quantitatively, did not (18:9-14).

The poor almost always find themselves outcasts, but Luke effectively shows Jesus standing up for them in a passage unfamiliar to many Christians. We all know the eight beatitudes from Matthew 5:1-10, including the famous, "Blessed are the poor in spirit, for theirs is the kingdom of heaven." It is a beautiful saying, but note that Matthew has "poor *in spirit,*" so this saying can apply to those who are not actually poor in money and goods. Furthermore, by using the third person, Matthew has Jesus enunciate an ethical principle.

Almost no one knows Luke's beatitudes (6:20-26), but there Jesus says, "Blessed are you *who are poor,* for yours is the kingdom of God" (v. 20). These people are poor, not "in spirit," but genuinely poor. Note also that instead of articulating ethical principles, Jesus speaks directly to them (*"you* who are poor"). Luke goes on in this same vein: "Blessed are *you who are hungry now,* for you will be filled" (v. 21). These people do not "hunger and thirst for righteousness" (Matt 5:6); they are without food now, and again Jesus speaks directly to them. Luke's presentation of the beatitudes is not the only instance of this concern for the impoverished. He returns to this theme in his well-known parable of the rich man and the beggar Lazarus (16:19-31).

Besides Gentiles, social outcasts, and the poor, Luke shows Jesus caring for women who, in that era, were routinely oppressed and abused. The evangelist repeatedly shows Jesus rising above the prejudices of his age. Luke alone tells how Jesus raised from the dead the "only son" of the widow of Nain (7:11-17). "Only" is the operative word because a widow who lost her only son would have no man to care for her, which in ancient society meant destitution. Luke is also the only evangelist to give credit to the women who financially supported Jesus and his disciples (8:1-3), no small kindness for people always on the move and in constant need of food and shelter. In the Acts of the Apostles, Luke tells of four un-named women who prophesy (21:9), of Priscilla who taught the faith (18:26), of the mother of John Mark (12:12) and the convert Lydia (16:14-15) who may have headed local house churches. But it is his infancy narrative in which Luke in-cludes his most important presentations of women—of Eliza-beth, of Anna, and especially of Jesus' mother Mary, the model disciple for this evangelist.

Even this brief sketch demonstrates that Matthew and Luke never overlooked or omitted the focus of the other's gospel. Just as Matthew's Jesus saves all people, Luke's Jesus respects the Law. But this sketch also demonstrates that the two evan-gelists offer their own portraits of Jesus, their own Christolo-gies. Just as Jesus the Jewish savior will dominate Matthew's infancy narrative, so Jesus the universal savior will dominate Luke's infancy narrative.

Let us now turn to those narratives.

CHAPTER THREE

Matthew's Infancy Narrative

Chapter 1

Every Christmas I envision a sincere believer who, sick of secular media hype and over-sentimentalized religious literature, decides to go back to the true sources, to read the gospel infancy narratives. That believer then takes up a Bible, turns to the New Testament, starts to read Matthew's gospel, and runs headlong into a genealogy. As my students would say, "Bor-r-r-ing," and they would be right.

But not 100 percent right. Like it or not, the genealogy makes up one-quarter of the infancy narrative, and we cannot understand that narrative without understanding why Matthew starts with it.

The Genealogy of Jesus (1:1-17)

(1) An account of the genealogy of Jesus the Messiah, the son of David, the son of Abraham.

(2) Abraham was the father of Isaac, and Isaac the father of Jacob, and Jacob the father of Judah and his brothers, (3) and Judah the father of Perez and Zerah by Tamar, and Perez the father of Hezron, and Hezron the father of Aram, (4) and Aram the father of Aminadab, and

Aminadab the father of Nahshon, and Nahshon the father of Salmon, (5) and Salmon the father of Boaz by Rahab, and Boaz the father of Obed by Ruth, and Obed the father of Jesse, (6) and Jesse the father of King David.

And David was the father of Solomon by the wife of Uriah, (7) and Solomon the father of Rehoboam, and Rehoboam the father of Abijah, and Abijah the father of Asaph, (8) and Asaph the father of Jehoshaphat, and Jehoshaphat the father of Joram, and Joram the father of Uzziah, (9) and Uzziah the father of Jotham, and Jotham the father of Ahaz, and Ahaz the father of Hezekiah, (10) and Hezekiah the father of Manasseh, and Manasseh the father of Amos, and Amos the father of Josiah, (11) and Josiah the father of Jechoniah and his brothers at the time of deportation to Babylon.

(12) And after the deportation to Babylon: Jechoniah was the father of Salathiel, and Salathiel the father of Zerubbabel, (13) and Zerubbabel the father of Abiud, and Abiud the father of Eliakim, and Eliakim the father of Azor, (14) and Azor the father of Zadok, and Zadok the father of Achim, and Achim the father of Eliud, (15) and Eliud the father of Eleazar, and Eleazar the father of Matthan, and Matthan the father of Jacob, (16) and Jacob the father of Joseph the husband of Mary, of whom Jesus was born, who is called the Messiah.

(17) So all the generations from Abraham to David are fourteen generations; and from David to the deportation to Babylon, fourteen generations; and from the deportation to Babylon to the Messiah, fourteen generations.

Genealogies are quite common in the ancient world, and Luke also provided one (3:23-38) for his readers, although he did not make it part of his infancy narrative. More to the point, the Hebrew Bible has many genealogies, and they appear very early on. For example, the fifth chapter of Genesis traces the line from Adam to Noah and his sons, while the tenth chapter traces the genealogies descending from Noah's sons, and the eleventh chapter gives us the genealogy of Abram (who becomes Abraham in chapter 17). So popular were genealogies that the first nine chapters of the First Book of Chronicles contain nothing but genealogies with more than 1,000 names—surely the least read and preached upon section of the entire Bible.

Let us look at a typical and famous genealogy, that of Ezra, the Jewish reformer who gave his name to one of the biblical books. His genealogy appears in Ezra 7:1-5: "Ezra son of Seriah, son of Azariah, son of Hilkiah, son of Shallum, son of Zadok, son of Ahitub, son of Amariah, son of Azariah, son of Meraioth, son of Zerahiah, son of Uzzi, son of Bukki, son of Abishua, son of Phinehas, son of Eleazar, son of the chief priest Aaron."

This list of Ezra's ancestors includes sixteen names, and what the modern person notices immediately is that all of them are men. Assuming the ancient Israelites did not reproduce asexually, we must ask what is going on here.

The answer is simple: patriarchy, a form of government that places all power in the hands of men and an attitude that considers women to be inferior in all aspects. The Jews and all ancient pagan peoples practiced patriarchy, and the Christians, too, adopted this, forbidding women to teach, telling them how to dress, and equating their value solely with their ability to bear children, especially sons (1 Tim 2:8-15)—this last point being one that plays an important role in Luke's infancy narrative. So we are not surprised that biblical genealogies focused on the male ancestors. Because of this, Matthew's gospel surprises us because his genealogy for Jesus includes five women, the last being Jesus' mother Mary.

Matthew starts with a strong nod to his Jewish-Christian readers: "An account of the genealogy of Jesus the Messiah, the son of David, the son of Abraham." He announces that Jesus was the one for whom the Jews had waited (although the gospel will make it clear that he was not a political Messiah), and then he shows that Jesus descended from David, the greatest of the Jewish kings, and ultimately from Abraham, the father of the Jewish people. By contrast, writing for a largely Gentile audience, Luke (3:38) traces Jesus' human genealogy back to Adam, father of the entire human race. [We must note that Matthew's genealogy does not completely exclude Gentiles since Genesis (12:3; 22:18) tells us that all the nations of the earth will be blessed in Abraham.]

After this formal beginning, Matthew lists the names. At verse 3 we read, "Judah the father of Perez and Zerah by Tamar," and at verses 5-6 we read, "and Salmon the father of Boaz by Rahab, and Boaz the father of Obed by Ruth, and Obed the father of Jesse, and Jesse the father of King David. And David was the father of Solomon by the wife of Uriah." [Uriah was a pagan, a Hittite, who served David as a mercenary warrior.] The preposition "by" introduces the mothers of these men, namely, Tamar, Rahab, Ruth, and the wife of Uriah the Hittite. Who were they?

For starters, Tamar, Rahab, and Ruth were definitely Gentiles. The wife of Uriah, Bathsheba, was a Jew, but Matthew identifies her via her Gentile husband. Jesus' mother was a Jew but, as we shall see, under some suspicion, so Matthew precedes her with women whose ethnic backgrounds or marital status made them different from what pious Jews would have suspected.

But the careers of these four OT women also made them unique.

In Genesis 38 we learn that the Hebrew patriarch Judah married his firstborn son Er to a woman named Tamar, who in Jewish tradition was a pagan but one willing to convert to the faith of Abraham. But the Lord struck Er dead for his wickedness, and, by tradition, Judah's next oldest son, Onan, had to marry his brother's widow so that they could produce a son who would carry on the deceased brother's bloodline. But Onan refused his responsibility in this matter, and so the

Lord struck him dead as well. Apprehensive that his third son Shelah would also die, Judah told Tamar to remain a widow, at least until Shelah grew up. Fearful that she would never have a son and thus be disgraced, Tamar suspected something was up, and she was right. When Shelah reached adulthood, Judah did not arrange a marriage for him with her. By now Judah was a widower, so Tamar clothed herself like a harlot and lured Judah into having relations with her. She became pregnant and proved to Judah that he was the father. He acknowledged that she and not he had acted rightly, and when she gave birth to twin sons, Perez and Zelah, Judah acknowledged them as his own. Perez became an ancestor of David.

Tamar pretended to be a harlot; Rahab was one. This Canaanite woman protected Joshua's spies (Josh 2) when they gathered information about Jericho. Neither the Old Testament nor Jewish tradition mentions her as the wife of Salmon and mother of Boaz, but she is the only woman named Rahab in the OT, and thus the only woman to whom Matthew can be referring.

According to the biblical book bearing her name, Ruth was a Moabite, widow of an Israelite, and she married another Israelite named Boaz. She is portrayed as a good woman, but one who had to be proactive in getting Boaz eventually to marry her. She became the grandmother of the great Israelite king David.

The wife of Uriah the Hittite is Bathsheba, whom King David lusted after when he saw her bathing (1 Sam 11:1–12:25). Kings usually got what they wanted, and he committed adultery with her. Apparently blaming only Bathsheba for this act, Matthew declines even to mention her name. But she became the mother of Solomon, the grand king of Israel and the builder of the temple.

Ancient readers would have been surprised, even mystified, that Matthew included women in his genealogy of Jesus, but, if this were the case, they would have expected these women to be significant figures of Jewish history, such as Sarah,

Rebecca, Rachel, Miriam, or Esther, appropriate role models leading up to Jesus' mother. But these four OT women had something unusual or irregular about them that would make them surprising inclusions in a genealogy of the Messiah. In spite of this, these women played important roles in advancing Israelite history: Tamar gave Judah two sons, one from whom David was descended; Rahab helped the Israelites capture Jericho; Ruth was the grandmother of David; and Bathsheba gave birth to Solomon. Mary likewise would play a crucial role in Jewish history but also in human history by giving birth to the Messiah. Yet she, too, was a woman about whom questions could be raised.

The Hebrew Bible contains many examples of women who overcame obstacles to give birth, such as Sarah, Rebecca, and the mothers of Samson and Samuel, and Luke's gospel includes the example of Elizabeth. In all these cases, the fathers of their sons were their husbands. But the early Christians made the startling assertion that Mary had conceived virginally. One can imagine the derision that this claim would have met among pagans and some Jews. By the second century a pagan writer named Celsus reports a Jewish claim that Jesus was the illegitimate son of a sinful village girl and a Roman soldier named Panthera. Did Matthew have this accusation in mind when he used these other misunderstood women in Jesus' genealogy?

We cannot be sure, but a clue may lie in Matthew's resurrection narrative (28:11-15). He says that after Jesus rose from the dead, the temple priests bribed the guards to say that his disciples had stolen his body. The guards did as they were told, "and this story is still told among the Jews *to this day*," that is, when Matthew was writing in the 80s of the first century. The evangelist wrote his resurrection account partially to counter some current Jewish claims about Jesus' resurrection. Were there equally damaging stories circulating about Jesus' birth when Matthew wrote?

Matthew also points out that this genealogy contains forty-two names, that is, three sets of fourteen. What is so important about the number fourteen? Frankly, not much, but seven was a sacred number, that of the first week of creation (Gen 1:1–2:4). This genealogy divided the time before Jesus to two weeks (= two sevens) from Abraham to David, two more from David the Babylonian Exile, and two weeks beyond that to Jesus who "thus begins the seventh period, the period of perfection and fulfillment" (Harrington, p. 18), at least according to Jewish apocalyptic speculation.

There is another possibility. The ancient Mediterranean peoples did not use Arabic numerals for numbers; instead they used letters to symbolize numbers. To a small extent, we still use Roman numerals, such as Queen Elizabeth II (= 2) or Super Bowl XXXV (= 35). Matthew emphasizes Jesus' Davidic descent (1:1; 1:6; 1:17; 1:20). In Hebrew, the numeric values of the letters of the name David is fourteen. But scholars simply cannot be sure if this is why Matthew chose that number.

The tradition of a virginal conception raises a problem for Matthew's genealogy. Several times in his gospel Jews recognize Jesus as the Son of David (9:27; 12:23; 21:9), a term that the evangelist uses of Joseph in the infancy narrative (1:20). But if Mary conceived virginally, then what difference does Joseph's Davidic descent make since he had nothing to do with fathering Jesus. That is true physically but not legally, that is, according to ancient Jewish law. To quote Raymond Brown, "Joseph can acknowledge Jesus by naming him, and that makes him 'Son of David.'" Matthew's ancient audience would have understood something that seems so puzzling to us. They also would have accepted that Joseph's act enabled Jesus to stand in the Davidic line and so be the Messiah.

PASTORAL REFLECTION

A genealogy does not appear to be a good topic for a pastoral consideration, but the ancient Jews, like Jesus, took them very seriously. For them, the genealogy had a physical base— bloodline traceable back to the founder of the Jewish people. For Christians, a genealogy reminds us that our faith began a long time ago, has matured over the centuries, and is still developing today. We have benefited from what previous generations of Christians have done, and future generations will benefit from what we do.

That is a scary prospect. It is one thing to look to past generations; something quite different to picture future generations looking toward us. We know how unworthy, how sinful we are, but we must always remember that every generation of Christians is exactly the same. Without sinners, Christianity would not exist. We should see ourselves as God sees us, as basically good people but with our flaws, sinners trying to do better, failing, and trying again. Previous generations struggled and somehow succeeded. If they had failed, we would not be Christian today. Let's take encouragement from them and do our best for the coming generations.

The Birth of Jesus (1:18-26)

(18) Now the birth of Jesus the Messiah took place in this way. When his mother Mary had been engaged to Joseph, but before they lived together, she was found to be with child from the Holy Spirit. (19) Her husband Joseph, being a righteous man and unwilling to expose her to public disgrace, planned to dismiss her quietly. (20) But just when he had resolved to do this, an angel of the Lord appeared to him in a dream and said, "Joseph, son of David, do not be afraid to take Mary as your wife, for the child conceived in her is from the Holy Spirit. (21) She will bear a son, and you are to name him Jesus, for he will save his people from their sins." (22) All this took place to fulfill what had been spoken by the Lord through the prophet: (23) "Look, the virgin shall conceive and bear a son, and they shall name him Emmanuel," which means "God is with us." (24) When Joseph awoke from sleep, he did as the angel of the Lord commanded him; he took her as his wife, (25) but had no

> *marital relations with her until she had borne a son; (26)*
> *and he named him Jesus.*

After the genealogy, Matthew turns to the actual birth in a matter-of-fact way: "Now the birth of Jesus took place in this way," going on to say that Mary and Joseph were "engaged but before they lived together." This requires some explanation of ancient Jewish marital customs.

A marriage involved two steps. First, the couple acknowledged their consent to the marriage, a process usually translated into English as "betrothal" but meaning more than the English word implies. The man had legal rights over the woman, and she was called his wife, which is how Mary is described in verses 1:20 and 1:24, and so any sexual relations between one partner and another person would be considered adultery. After the betrothal, the couple lived apart, usually in their parents' homes, for a year, after which the man took the woman to his home, provided support for her and protected her (as Joseph did at the time Herod wished to kill Jesus). At this point the two could legally engage in conjugal relations. At the time of the announcement to Joseph by the angel, Mary and he had already become betrothed but were not yet living together.

But "she was found to be with child from the Holy Spirit." Joseph felt that he must break off the engagement on the grounds of adultery. Matthew says Joseph was a righteous man, which means that he observed the precepts of the Law, but he also cared for Mary and did not wish to expose her to embarrassment and the certain social fate of never being able to get married. As John's gospel demonstrates (8:1-11), an adulteress even ran the risk of being stoned to death by a mob. Joseph decided to "dismiss her quietly," a very merciful step to take for a man convinced that his betrothed had betrayed him. The gospel says nothing of Joseph's personal desolation at this sad prospect.

Aside from this merciful act, Matthew does not tell us any-thing about Joseph, who literally disappears from the gospel after the infancy narrative. At 13:55, some anonymous Jews ask, "Is this man (Jesus) not the carpenter's son?" so we know Joseph's profession. Several gospel passages record that Mary was alive during Jesus' public ministry, but none men-tions Joseph at those times, so apparently he had died before Jesus began his ministry. Aside from this little bit, we know nothing of Joseph's life.

But in this infancy narrative he plays a central role because "an angel of the Lord appeared to him in a *dream*." This dream is the first of five which Matthew will include in his infancy narrative (1:20; 2:12; 2:13; 2:19; 2:22). Why did he include dreams? First, because in the ancient world gods rou-tinely communicated with people in dreams, and so did the one deity of the Jews. In dreams God spoke to Abraham (Gen 20:3), to Jacob (Gen 28:12), and to Solomon (1 Kgs 3:5). God also helped his servants to interpret the dreams of others, as Daniel interpreted the dreams of the Babylonian king Nebu-chadnezzar (Dan 2). Matthew's readers would readily accept this as a medium of divine communication.

Second, the most famous interpreter of dreams in the He-brew Bible was Joseph's namesake, the Hebrew patriarch Jo-seph who, while a prisoner in an Egyptian jail, interpreted the dreams of Pharaoh (Gen 39–41). Furthermore, Jesus' father Joseph is the only man in the gospels who goes to Egypt.

We might be surprised that God did not speak to Joseph but rather an angel did, but that, too, would resonate positively with Matthew's readers. The Greek word *ángelos* means sim-ply "messenger," and throughout the Old Testament God uses these messengers. We could look at many examples, but just one will conclusively illustrate the point. "Moses was keeping the flock of his father-in-law Jethro, the priest of Midian; he led his flock beyond the wilderness, and came to Horeb, the mountain of God. There the *angel of the* Lord appeared to him in a flame of fire out of a bush; he looked, and the bush was blazing, yet it was not consumed" (Exod 3:1-2). An angel could bear the earthly manifestation of the Lord in the call of Moses, one of the most decisive events in Israelite history, so the angel in this gospel dream would have all the authenticity any reader could want. It would also reinforce the comparison Matthew wished to make between Moses and Jesus.

The angel told Joseph that Mary had conceived by the Holy Spirit, although not how. This is a miracle, but one that surpasses the miraculous births of so many Old Testament figures like Isaac, Sampson, and Samuel. Matthew here stresses not only Jesus' continuity with but also his superiority to the major figures of the Old Testament. Now Joseph could marry Mary with a good conscience. From this pregnancy would come a son who will be named Jesus, the Greek form of the Hebrew name Joshua and a name that meant "savior." Most Christians know of the annunciation of Jesus' birth to Mary by the angel Gabriel, who tells Mary the child's name (Luke 1:31). That fits Luke's empowering of women, but the more traditional Matthew has the unnamed angel give the name to the man, who in turn (1:21) will actually name the boy. (Since this gospel does not include an annunciation to Mary, at no point does Matthew relate how she found out what had occurred.) And while Luke provides many predictions of Jesus' career, Matthew notes simply that "he will save his people from their sins" (1:21). The phrase "his people" refers to the Jews and Gentile Christians for whom Matthew was writing.

Matthew goes on to say that the conception of Jesus by the power of the Holy Spirit fulfills a prophecy, Isaiah 7:14, which the evangelist renders: "Look, the virgin shall conceive and bear a son, and they shall name him Emmanuel" (Matt 1:23). In his infancy narrative, he cites five prophecies (1:23; 2:6; 2:15; 2:18; 2:23), which we would expect an evangelist writing for many Jewish converts to do. But this, the most famous of the prophecies, presents some real problems.

The problems start with the Hebrew text of Isaiah 7:14, which reads: "Behold, a *young woman* shall conceive and bear a son, and *she* shall call him Emmanuel." Let us examine this famous text and its use in the gospel.

1.   First of all, Matthew misquotes the text. Isaiah says "she" (the mother) will call the child "Emmanuel," not, as Matthew has it, that "they" would call him that. And who are "they"? Normally a pronoun refers back to the nearest previous noun. In this case, it would be the word "people" in 1:21, so Matthew has those saved by Jesus, both Jewish and Gentile converts, acknowledge him as Emmanuel or "God with us." Maybe not Isaiah's exact text but a strong theological insight.

2.   Second, Matthew cites Isaiah in Greek, but even in Greek the prophet does not explicitly refer to a virginal conception. But that raises another question—Isaiah was written in Hebrew. Where did Matthew get a Greek version of it?

As we saw in chapter 1, after the conquests of Alexander the Great, Greek became a common language in the near East, and many Jews migrated to Greek-speaking cities like Alexandria in Egypt. By the third century BC, the Alexandrian Jews had begun to lose contact with the Hebrew language and wanted a translation of the Bible into the language they then spoke. Scholars debate many aspects of the translation of the Hebrew Bible into Greek, but they agree that it started in Alexandria. The text soon became the equivalent of the original Bible to the Diasporan Jews, much the way many conservative English-speaking Christians treat the King James Version. So sacred did the Greek text become that by the second century BC a legend grew up about the translation, which was supposed to have been done miraculously by seventy-two translators, and the text acquired the name Septuagint or "work of the Seventy," a less cumbersome title than "the work of the seventy-two."

The Septuagint text says that "a virgin will conceive," that is, a woman who is now a virgin will at some point conceive, presumably by conjugal relations with her husband, which is how the ancient Jews read the text. But both Matthew and Luke, who does *not* cite Isaiah, witness to a unique and very early Christian belief in a virginal conception. Matthew did not create the virginal conception but rather cited an OT passage from a Greek text to support his belief. Ancient Jews could not accept this; it is a matter of Christian faith, and the gospels proclaim the faith of the church in Christ.

Third, and most problematically—at least on the surface—is that the Hebrew text of Isaiah does not use the word for "virgin" but rather the word for "young woman." Why? Many carping and unlearned critics have accused Matthew of duplicity, of knowingly changing the text. They also accuse modern Christians of refusing to acknowledge what Isaiah really said. But none of that is true.

In the New Testament books, quotations from the Hebrew Bible appear in Greek and are usually from the Septuagint. This is crucial to Matthew because when the Septuagint translators turned Isaiah 7:14 into Greek, these Jewish translators used the word for "virgin" to translate the Hebrew "young girl." By the time Matthew wrote his gospel, Diasporan Jews had been reading the Septuagint "A virgin shall conceive" for almost three centuries. Contrary to the critics, the early Christians did not change Isaiah's text but rather made use of a centuries-old *Jewish* translation.

Fourth, in spite of Matthew's prediction that "they (the people) will call him Emmanuel, which means 'God is with us'," the name does not appear anywhere else in the New Testament, not even in Matthew's own gospel, although he alludes to it in his final verse (28:20) in which Jesus says: "And remember, *I am with you* always, to the end of the age." This will not be the only time that Matthew connects the beginning and end of Jesus' time on earth.

Although Matthew cites five prophecies in his infancy narrative, this one from Isaiah has been the best known and, at times, the most controversial, but the evangelist considered it important to quote this particular prophet. Isaiah had great importance for early Christians. For example, the apostle Paul made thirty-seven quotations from the Israelite prophets

in his epistles, and twenty-seven of them are from the book of
Isaiah. In the infancy narrative Matthew cites Isaiah a second
time (v. 2:11 citing Isa 60:6). Isaiah also appears frequently in
Matthew's gospel outside of the infancy narratives.

Let us return to the narrative. "Joseph awoke from his
dream" and, following the angelic instructions, married Mary,
"but had no marital relations with her until she had borne a
son; and he named him Jesus." Debate grew up around the
phrase "no marital relations with her *until* she had borne a
son." By the second century, Christians in Syria had begun to
teach that Jesus' mother Mary had maintained her virginity
for her entire lifetime, that is, that Joseph and she never had
conjugal relations. Critics of this position argued that this
phrase implies just the reverse, that is, that Mary and Joseph
had relations after Jesus' birth.

Not surprisingly, in unecumenical ages, this scholarly debate took on confessional and denominational overtones.
Modern scholarship—Catholic, Protestant, and Orthodox—
has concluded that the Greek of the text means only that
Joseph and Mary did not have relations prior to Jesus' birth.
This verse says nothing about either perpetual virginity or
subsequent conjugal relations, which in later centuries became doctrinal issues. Churches are not bound solely to the
biblical text and can develop their own doctrines from it, but
our concern here is Matthew's infancy narrative and not how
this verse was understood long after he wrote.

A final note before we head to chapter 2. Nowhere in chapter 1 does Matthew mention where Mary and Joseph lived.
Most Christians assume it was Nazareth because of Luke's
infancy narrative, but Matthew says nothing about it in this
chapter.

PASTORAL REFLECTION

Although Joseph plays a major role in this passage, note
that he never says a word—not just here but literally nowhere

in the gospels. Thanks to endless artistic portrayals of the Virgin and Child, we have vivid images of Jesus and his mother, but Joseph remains in the shadows. The doctrine of the virginal conception further diminishes his role since, in modern eyes (if not ancient Jewish ones), he is not truly Jesus' father but rather a man there to care for Mary and her son. Think of the many artistic representations of the Nativity that show Joseph sitting off to the side or even asleep. Artists did this to emphasize the virginal conception by showing Joseph having nothing to do with the conception and birth.

Oddly enough, Joseph's relative unimportance makes him a realistic model for us. How many of us are or will be great figures of the faith? The uncharismatic Joseph was a righteous man, that is, a good Jew, one who knew and practiced his faith. He did not need to be a great figure, just a good one who was there when others needed him. He did not need words to memorialize him; deeds proved sufficient. He was quietly religious, as most people are. He was a layperson, not a member of the temple priesthood, and he saw his vocation as a Jew to be a good spouse and a good parent.

Thanks to my parents, Joseph is my namesake, and I hope that I have been and continue to be a good spouse and a good parent, worthy callings in any era.

Chapter 2

Although the infancy narratives make up only two of twenty-eight chapters in Matthew's gospel, most scholars believe that he did not write a consecutive infancy account but rather joined together traditions familiar to him. That is because of the mysterious magi from the East, who, with no previous notice, abruptly appear in chapter 2 and take up twelve of its twenty-three verses, while the consequences of their visit take up the rest of the chapter. This sudden change in the narrative makes sense if we recognize that Matthew, writing almost ninety years after Jesus' birth, had to record and organize some old and probably less-than-clear traditions. He succeeded brilliantly. People who know nothing of Jesus' genealogy still know of the magi and the star that led them to the newborn king.

The Visit of the Magi (2:1-12)

(1) In the time of King Herod, after Jesus was born in Bethlehem of Judea, wise men from the East came to Jerusalem, (2) asking, "Where is the child who has been born king of the Jews? For we observed his star at its rising, and have come to pay him homage." (3) When King Herod heard this, he was frightened, and all Jerusalem with him; (4) and calling together all the chief priests and scribes of the people, he inquired of them where the Messiah was to be born. (5) They told him, "In Bethlehem of Judea; for so it has been written by the prophet: (6) 'And you, Bethlehem, in the land of Judah, are by no means least among the rulers of Judah; for from you shall come a ruler who is to shepherd my people Israel.'"

(7) Then Herod secretly called for the wise men and learned from them the exact time when the star had appeared. (8) Then he sent them to Bethlehem, saying, "Go and search diligently for the child; and when you have found him, bring me word so that I may also go and pay him homage." (9) When they had heard the king, they set out; and there, ahead of them, went the star that they had seen at its rising, until it stopped over the place where the child was. (10) When they saw that the star had stopped, they were overwhelmed with joy. (11) On entering the house, they saw the child with Mary his mother; and they knelt down and paid him homage. Then, opening their treasure chests, they offered him gifts of gold, frankincense, and myrrh. (12) And having been warned in a dream not to return to Herod, they left for their own country by another road.

The evangelist offered no chronological or geographical setting in chapter 1, but here he starts off with both: "In the time of King Herod, after Jesus was born in Bethlehem of Judea. . . ." (2:1). Let us first consider Bethlehem.

Matthew and Luke agree that Jesus was born there, but Luke cites a Roman census to get Jesus' parents from Nazareth of Galilee to Bethlehem of Judea, whereas Matthew simply says he was born there. Someone who had not read about the census in Luke would naturally conclude that Jesus was born in Bethlehem because that is where his parents lived. But what about Nazareth? Matthew knows that Jesus grew up there, but he says that occurred because Joseph migrated there after the Holy Family left Egypt (2:22-23).

Most Christians have put the two infancy narratives together and assume that Mary and Joseph lived in Nazareth, went to Bethlehem to register for the census, and then, after a sojourn in Egypt, returned to Nazareth. But forcing the narratives together simply does not work. Why would Matthew have left out the census if that was how Jesus' parents came to be in Bethlehem? And how could Luke have left out the magi, the attempt to murder Jesus, and the Holy Family's flight into Egypt? And even if one could possibly believe that the two evangelists left out such stunning material, we still need to explain why in Matthew's gospel Joseph needed an angelic dream to decide to go to Nazareth of Galilee if that was where he had lived before fleeing to Egypt.

The problems of forcing the two narratives together extend beyond the place of birth. For example, recall that Matthew has the annunciation of Jesus' birth given to Joseph while Luke has it given to Mary. Although Luke does not include his genealogy of Jesus (3:23-38) in his infancy narrative, we can still compare the two and see how very different they are. Recall further that the two evangelists differ with the wording of the Lord's Prayer and of the beatitudes. The conclusion is inescapable. Matthew and Luke simply did not know one another's gospels. We can say for sure that Jesus was born in

Bethlehem and grew up in Nazareth, but we must interpret the two infancy narratives on their own.

In addition to being Jesus' birthplace, Bethlehem was the home of David (1 Sam 17:12), thus reminding Matthew's Jewish converts and us of Jesus' genealogy.

Matthew introduces King Herod, also known as Herod the Great, who ruled Judea for the Romans. Contrary to what most movies portray, the Romans did not persecute their subject peoples. They wanted what all imperialists want, peace and taxes. Where possible, they ruled through local monarchs or nobility who might be more acceptable to the subjects than a Roman governor would be and who would know and understand local customs. This approach succeeded brilliantly. Given the size of the empire and how long the Romans ruled, they experienced very few revolts.

The Romans conquered Palestine in 63 BC. The Jewish leaders did not accept the conquest easily, and struggles ensued. A Gentile adventurer named Antipater, who was (nominally) a Jew religiously, quickly became a man the Romans could count on. In 47 Antipater named his 26-year-old son Herod to be governor of Galilee. Patronized by Mark Antony, in 37 Herod became king of Judea (the Roman province), and he ruled until 4 BC. A clever, vicious, devious man, Herod survived the fall of Mark Antony (who ignored Herod's advice to kill Cleopatra), and he won the trust of Augustus, emperor of Rome until AD 14.

Convinced of his greatness, Herod built and built—fortresses, stadiums, theaters, and most importantly, the temple in Jerusalem to replace the one built by Solomon and destroyed the Babylonians in the sixth century BC. It was one of the wonders of the ancient Near East and never failed to impress rustic visitors such as Jesus' disciples (Luke 21:5). But Herod never took the Jewish religion seriously, observing it only in public, which never really fooled the Jews.

Herod ruled like a tyrant, and like most tyrants, he saw plots everywhere. He had scores of people assassinated and did not spare even members of his own family. He had one of his wives and three of his sons murdered. Only Matthew tells us of the massacre of the innocents in Bethlehem, but his account fits Herod's character.

The observant reader may have caught a serious chronological problem. Herod died in 4 BC, but Jesus was born during his reign. How could Christ be born four years before Christ? The answer is quite simple. In the sixth century a Syrian monk named Dionysius Exiguus prepared a new calendar based on the now familiar BC-AD schema. On that calendar Jesus should have been born exactly as the era turned from BC to AD, but Dionysius miscalculated the date of Herod's death. By the time later scholars caught the mistake, the calendar had been in place for centuries.

Actually, Jesus could have been born as early as 6 BC. At 2:7 Matthew tells us that Herod asked the magi for "the exact time when the star had appeared," and at 2:16 Herod orders the execution of all boys "who were two years old or under," thus showing that Herod had reason to believe the child could have been as old as two. Since Herod died in 4 BC, this means Jesus could have been born as early as 6 BC.

Matthew packs a lot in verse 2:1. In addition to learning that Jesus was born in Bethlehem and Herod ruled at the time, we learn of the "wise men [= magi] from the East." We all know who they were: three kings named Melchior, Caspar, and Balthasar, who rode camels to visit Jesus. Actually, none of that appears in the Bible. Later tradition made them kings, gave them names, put them astride camels, and yes, even determined that there were three of them, probably because there were three gifts.

If that is what tradition tells us, then what does Matthew himself tell us? The Greek word *mágos* originally meant a priest of the Zoroastrian religion, the official religion of ancient Persia, which today is Iran. Certainly this designation fits Matthew's "from the East." Additionally, the Persian magi practiced astrology as did the gospel magi who left their

homes and country to follow a star. But in the first century
the word *mágos* could also mean anyone who practiced not
just astrology but also divination, fortune telling, and magic,
a word with the same root as magi. In the Acts of the
Apostles (8:9-24), Peter has a contest with Simon Magus, that
is, Simon the *mágos*, a cynical and opportunistic magician
who offers Peter money to learn how to do the "tricks" (miracles) Simon had just seen Peter do.

Since the magi traveled far to venerate Jesus as a king,
clearly Matthew means the word in a positive way, probably
as Persian astrologers.

Matthew also has the Hebrew Bible in mind. In the book of
Numbers a seer named Balaam had agreed to the wishes of a
pagan king to curse the people Israel, but a talking donkey
and a stern angel (Num 22:22-35) got him to change his
mind. He blessed Israel and predicted (24:17) that "a star
shall come out of Jacob." Matthew's readers would have
known about Balaam and his prophecy and thus appreciated
the evangelist's link of star and seer. But there is more. A
great Diasporan Jewish scholar, an Alexandrian named Philo
(ca. 20 BC–ca. AD 50), referred to Balaam as a *mágos*, which
strengthens the connection between the pagan seer and the
mysterious visitors.

The magi tell Herod they have come to pay homage to the
newborn "king of the Jews." That was the title the Romans
had given to Herod, who immediately saw a threat to his
reign. Frightened at this prospect and assuming the newborn
king to be the Messiah, Herod has his court scholars and the
chief priests search the Hebrew Bible to find out where the
Messiah would be born. They tell him Bethlehem, which fulfills Micah 5:2, the second prophecy Matthew cites.

Next comes a historically puzzling account. Herod calls the
magi to him secretly, tells them to search for the child, and
when they have found him, to report back to Herod so that he,
too, might pay homage to the newborn king. But why would a
ruthless, devious, frightened tyrant like Herod entrust his

throne to these strangers? Why would he not go with them or send some of his assassins with them or at least have the magi followed? And would the magi have so naively believed that a sitting king would do homage to a child who could threaten his throne? Matthew wrote ninety years after Jesus' birth, and we cannot be surprised that he did not get all of his facts in order.

But off the magi did go, following the star until it stopped over "the house" (2:11), not as in some later traditions, a cave. They gave Jesus gifts of gold, frankincense, and myrrh. Why did they offer these particular gifts?

Gold has an obvious relevance. Kings wanted wealth, and gold was a normal tribute. Court ceremonies often used frankincense, and so that gift also had royal overtones. It was also very rare, gotten from a resin of Arabian trees that legend said were guarded by winged serpents. Myrrh had different significance. Ancient pagans used it as a perfume, but Matthew's Jewish convert readers would see as something else—a spice used in burials, including the burial of Jesus (John 19:39). On the surface, that is hardly the kind of gift to give to an infant, but Matthew had something else in mind.

When we recall that the feast of Christmas did not exist in the first century and that the infancy narratives served as introductions to the entire gospels, the gift makes sense as Matthew again links Jesus' birth and death. In his epistle to the Romans (ch. 5), the apostle Paul had portrayed Jesus as the new Adam, and here Matthew tells of a birth that will result in a death that will destroy the death that Adam brought into the world. The evangelist uses the gift of myrrh to remind his readers why Jesus was born. In the simple words of the beautiful Appalachian Christmas hymn "I Wonder as I Wander," "Jesus the savior is come for to die."

But Matthew is also working other themes. Herod and the Jerusalem leaders want to kill Jesus while Gentiles want to venerate him. Matthew parallels this in his Passion narrative. Alone among the evangelists he tells the story of Pilate's wife (27:19), a Gentile who never met Jesus but who learns of him *in a dream*, directly parallel to the dreams of the magi. Pilate's wife tries to stop her husband from harming Jesus, but he ignores her and orders Jesus' execution, just as Herod, indifferent to the announcement of the infant king's birth by a star, tries to kill Jesus. Here the evangelist pointedly proclaims that Gentiles were open to Jesus and his message while the Jewish leadership was not, a central theme of his gospel. Note that Matthew does not equate the Jewish leadership with the Jewish people.

Matthew uses the star of Bethlehem to set up yet another parallel, a natural sign announcing a great event, which was a common literary device in ancient writing. Biographies of ancient Gentile kings and rulers routinely reported that unusual events occurred at their births, often some kind of sign in the heavens. But the evangelist is thinking beyond the story of Jesus' birth; he again links Jesus' birth and death.

When Jesus is born, a star announces the birth; when he dies, the sky becomes dark, which Mark and Luke also record, but only Matthew tells of the earthquake (27:51). Just as the natural world announced Jesus' birth, so it acknowledged his death. We may also find here another echo of the apostle Paul's Christology. Paul claimed that anyone could recognize God's existence via the created, natural world (Rom 1:19-20).

After giving their gifts, the magi were warned in a dream (Matthew's second) not to return to Herod, and so they returned home by a different route from the one they had taken (2:12). With that the magi passed into history, but they had a great future before them in legend.

Still, we cannot bid farewell to the magi without asking one "modern" question: was the star physically real or was it meant solely to remind Matthew's readers of Balaam and "star rising out of Jacob" and to parallel another celestial phenomenon like the eclipse at Jesus' death? One answer to that question is that the star could be both real and symbolic, as, for example, the cross of Jesus is both true wood but a lasting sign of human redemption.

A second answer would be that Matthew did indeed have in mind an actual, physical celestial phenomenon, yet it could not have been a star because stars do not move and stop or disappear and reappear. If not a star, then what? Modern astronomers have argued that at the time Jesus was born (6–4 BC), several planets were conjoining and making a bright sign in the sky. Furthermore, Korean astronomers recorded a supernova in 5 BC. Matthew likely knew that a celestial phenomenon had occurred about the time of Jesus' birth, and so, logically for his historical period, he understood it as a sign of a sacred event, namely Jesus' birth.

PASTORAL REFLECTION

In the infancy narratives, the magi are the only Gentiles to recognize Jesus. The word "Gentiles" really means "foreigners" or, most pointedly, "those outside the community." For most ancient Jews, "Gentiles" was an offensive term.

Christians believe theirs to be the true faith, but too many of us do so in an exclusivist way—"we're right; therefore they must be wrong." The first person to respond to this arrogant attitude was a second-century Palestinian Christian known to history as Justin the Martyr (d. ca. 165), who wondered how pagan Greek philosophers could have reasoned their way to one deity and had come up with strong ethical systems. Justin believed that all truth came from one source, the Word of God, so clearly the Word had worked through these Greek thinkers. Justin concluded that all people somehow share in the Divine Word, but that Christians enjoy its fullness because we have the Word incarnate in Jesus.

Justin's approach still has value. Do we really believe that God withholds his Word from one billion Muslims? From almost a billion Hindus? From a half-a-billion Buddhists? From Native Americans? From primitive peoples? Do we really believe that God who promised to be with Abraham's descendants to the end of time (Gen 17:7) has deserted the Jews? Does God break his promises?

Some people would reply, "OK, OK, so we'll be tolerant," but let us consider that word " tolerant." What does it mean? It means we "tolerate" what others believe, that is, it is all right for us if they believe. This sounds all right, but remember, we can always withdraw our tolerance.

The beliefs of others deserve our respect, not our toleration. This does not mean that we must agree totally with their beliefs—how can we?—but it does mean that we must accept that however full Christian revelation may be, God will always speak in many ways to many peoples, God's Word always deserves a hearing from us, and we must respect that Word and the people to whom it is given.

The Flight to Egypt, the Massacre of the Innocents, and the Return (2:13-23)

(13) Now after they had left, an angel of the Lord appeared to Joseph in a dream and said, "Get up, take the child and his mother, and flee to Egypt, and remain there until I tell you; for Herod is about to search for the child, to destroy him." (14) Then Joseph got up, took the child and his mother by night, and went to Egypt, (15) and remained there until the death of Herod. This was to fulfill what had been spoken by the Lord through the prophet, "Out of Egypt I have called my son."

(16) When Herod saw that he had been tricked by the wise men, he was infuriated, and he sent and killed all the children in and around Bethlehem who were two years old or under, according to the time that he had learned from the wise men. (17) Then was fulfilled what had been spoken through the prophet Jeremiah: (18) "A voice was heard in Ramah, wailing and loud lamentation, Rachel weeping for her children; she refused to be consoled, because they are no more."

(19) When Herod died, an angel of the Lord suddenly appeared in a dream to Joseph in Egypt and said, (20) "Get

> *up, take the child and his mother, and go to the land of Israel, for those who were seeking the child's life are dead." (21) Then Joseph got up, took the child and his mother, and went to the land of Israel. (22) But when he heard that Archelaus was ruling over Judea in place of his father Herod, he was afraid to go there. And after being warned in a dream, he went away to the district of Galilee. (23) There he made his home in a town called Nazareth, so that what had been spoken through the prophets might be fulfilled, "He will be called a Nazorean."*

Knowing Herod will not fail to act, Matthew's readers would expect the narrative to move quickly, and it does. In the first verse of this passage (2:13), an angel warns Joseph *in a dream* to take the child and his mother and flee to Egypt, that is, the Roman province of Aegyptus, to escape Herod's wrath and to remain there until the king's death. As it happens, this would also fulfill a prophecy, Hosea 11:1, "Out of Egypt I called my son," the third Matthean prophecy, here linked to the third Matthean dream.

Matthew turns briefly from the Holy Family to tell of Herod's rage at the magi's tricking him and how he tries to kill the newborn king (2:16-18). Herod has his soldiers kill all the boys in Bethlehem and the surrounding area who are under the age of two. Christian tradition has appropriately named these innocent victims the Holy Innocents and honors them with a feast day, December 28. And, Matthew being Matthew, this fulfills a prophecy, Jeremiah 31:15, with Rachel, a symbol of Israel, here being a symbol of the dead children's mothers.

But this episode has another consequence for understanding Jesus. Matthew says that Herod wanted to kill all boys "two years old or under, according to the time that he had learned from the wise men." This means that when the magi encountered Herod, the child could have been as much as two years old. Since modern scholars use Matthew's account to determine the date of Jesus' birth, they will, as we noted earlier, often place the event between 6 and 4 BC.

Matthew now turns to the Holy Family in Egypt. Jesus, Mary, and Joseph have become refugees fleeing oppression and violence, a sorrowful but immediate image for so many people in the modern world. Matthew himself does not develop this theme, and for two millennia Christians have focused more on the exotic nature of Egypt than on the sad state of the Holy Family.

The flight and residence in Egypt have fascinated visual artists, especially from the Renaissance to the nineteenth century. Dozens of fanciful, romanticized paintings portray the Holy Family with the pyramids in the background, effectively showing the bringer of a new age against the background of the greatest symbols of the ancient pagan world. Alas, this picture is not true, not even a little. Matthew does not give a location in Egypt, but recall that many Jews had migrated from the Holy Land to Alexandria and formed a community there. Joseph would have taken the same path, following a well-worn, reliable road to a city where, as Jews, his family and he would fit in and even be welcomed, and where he could find work. There is simply no reason why Joseph would have taken his family hundreds of miles down to the Nile to completely pagan territory where they would have been unfamiliar and unwanted.

Matthew, however, also has a strong symbolic interest in Egypt. Recall that he liked to parallel Jesus with Moses as he did in the Sermon on the Mount. Consider the parallels to the infancy accounts of both. A wicked king (pharaoh, Herod) fears a threat to his throne. He decides to kill all the boys of the ethnic group (Hebrews) or locale (Bethlehem) where this boy might be. Many innocent boys do die, but the chosen one survives. In a reverse parallel, later in his life Moses must flee from Egypt, while Jesus' family flees to Egypt.

Matthew even parallels the very language of the Exodus with his own narrative. "When Herod died, an angel of the Lord suddenly appeared in a dream to Joseph in Egypt and said, 'Get up, take the child and his mother, and go to the land of Israel, *for those who were seeking the child's life are dead*'" (Matt 2:19-20). Note the words of Exodus 4:19: "The LORD said to Moses in Midian, 'Go back to Egypt, *for all those who were seeking your life are dead.*'"

The evangelist immediately reinforces this image: "*Then Joseph got up, took the child and his mother, and went to the land of Israel*" (Matt 2:21); "*So Moses took his wife and his sons*, put them on a donkey *and went back to the land of Egypt*" (Exod 4:20). Note also that Matthew has Joseph return to the land of Israel, using the ancient name, rather the current, Roman names (Iudaea and Galilaea).

But more is at work here than just what the Bible says. Flavius Josephus (ca. AD 37–ca. 100), a Jewish historian, wrote a history of the Jews, adding material not found in the Bible. In his account of Moses in Egypt, Josephus records a Jewish tradition that one of pharaoh's "sacred scribes" told him that a child would soon be born who would threaten his rule, prompting pharaoh to kill the Hebrew boys. Matthew links the scribes (26:57; 27:41) with the "elders and chief priests" who bring about the death of Jesus, combining the Moses/Jesus parallel and the birth/death link. The evangelist's Jewish-Christian readers would have easily understood this very forceful and effective comparison.

The Matthean passage with the Exodus parallel occurs in a dream, the fourth, and Joseph, of course, obeys it. "But when he heard that Archelaus was ruling over Judea in place of his father Herod, he was afraid to go there. And after being warned in a dream, he went away to the district of Galilee. There he made his home in a town called Nazareth" (2:22-23). Rather surprisingly to many Christians, Nazareth appears for the first time in history in Mark's gospel. The Old Testament literally mentions it nowhere, nor does it appear in

Paul's epistles. Its insignificance probably lies behind the disciple Nathanael's wisecrack, "Can anything good come out of Nazareth?" as reported by the evangelist John (1:46).

Did Joseph choose an obscure town in Galilee—a region not ruled by Herod's son Archelaus—as a safe place for his threatened son? If so, he made a smart choice. Although not as bloody as his father, Archelaus brutally mistreated both his own people and the Samaritans, mocked Jewish marital morality with his affairs, and affronted reverence for the temple by arranging for a political crony to become the high priest. In AD 6 the Romans removed Archelaus from office, banished him to Gaul (modern France), and replaced him with a Roman procurator.

Whatever the historical situation, Matthew has a theological explanation, quickly paralleling the fifth dream with the fifth prophecy, that Joseph brought the family to Nazareth, "so that what had been spoken through the prophets might be fulfilled, 'He will be called a Nazorean.'"

Matthew has forced things a bit with this prophecy which comes not from a prophet but from "the prophets," whom he does not name. The most likely references are Isaiah 4:3 and Judges 13:3-7 and 16:17. Although the latter is not a formal prophetic book, the Jews include it among the books labeled "Prophets." Furthermore, since Nazareth was so obscure, most Jews would assume the word "Nazorean" meant a Nazirite, a man who had set himself aside as called by God and who abstained from wine, avoided touching corpses, and did not cut his hair (Num 6:1-21). In fact, Matthew's reference to Judges 16:17 is from the story of the long-haired Samson, who in this verse tells Delilah that he was Nazirite. All four gospels and the Acts of the Apostles attest that Jesus came from Nazareth. Matthew definitely means that the family settled there, but he still sees prophetic fulfillment, albeit with a little forcing of the OT text.

PASTORAL REFLECTION

I, a college-educated white American, am writing this passage in the comfort of my suburban Cleveland home where my wife and I do not worry about having clothes to wear or food to eat nor do we worry about our personal safety where we live. Our situation stands in stark contrast to how millions of our fellow human beings live. The computer on which I am working costs more than what 40 percent of the world's population receives for an annual income, and this is no special computer. We give to charity, but, in truth, we do not give what we could or should.

Thanks to Herod, the Holy Family must flee from their home; to use modern terms, they have become refugees from political violence. They have no home anymore, they flee to a foreign land, and they must depend upon the kindness of others, which, fortunately, they apparently received. But they cannot go back home because they still fear for their lives and that of their son since another tyrant has replaced the one they fled. They eventually settle in a different place, Galilee instead of Judea. Were they always welcome there?

If the Holy Family returned to earth today, with whom would they identify? Certainly not me or readers like me. They would identify with the wretched of this world who suffer injustice on a daily basis, who can never escape the threat of violence, whose rights mean nothing to their government, whose homes and persons are not secure. And what we can say about such people in general can be multiplied for women who, in many societies, count for little, have few rights, often suffer marital and sexual abuse, and, like the women of Bethlehem, witness the terrible deaths of their sons.

When my children were young, I told them that Christmas will always be our favorite holiday, but that it also has a sad note to it: good children whom Santa does not visit, people sitting around a table with little to eat, people not sitting around a table because there is no one for them to sit with. We give more generously to charity at that time of year, sometimes help people more personally and more directly, and at Christmas dinner ask God's blessing on those who do not have enough to eat. I know that many readers do likewise. But maybe it would help us all at Christmas to read the infancy narratives in their entirety, including the account of the Holy Family after the magi's departure. Maybe then we can more readily see the other members of the Holy Family in our own era.

When we recall that Matthew set out less to give a detailed historical account of Jesus' birth than to provide a Christological introduction to his gospel, we can see that he succeeded brilliantly. Major themes of the gospel make their first appearance here. For his Jewish-Christian readers, he portrays a Jewish Jesus with pious parents and with a genealogy running through David back to Abraham. Matthew parallels Jesus to Moses, cites fulfillment of prophecies, and includes details such as having the angel announce the birth to the man, not the woman, as would have been expected by Jews of that era. Furthermore, the main character of chapter 1 is Joseph, a Jew. But Matthew also opens the narrative to all people by making the pagan, Gentile magi the central figures of chapter 2 when they come to venerate Jesus. Nor does he ever separate these two groups. Matthew wrote after the apostle Paul realized that God's work through the people Israel continued in the universal church, and so this infancy narrative speaks to both Jew and Gentile, united in their new faith.

Perhaps most important, Matthew has established the major Christological point that moved him to write his infancy narrative: Jesus was always recognized as God's Son, right from his birth and indeed at his very conception.

CHAPTER FOUR

Luke's Infancy Narrative

Chapter 1

Luke's infancy narrative, like Matthew's, has an unexpected beginning. Readers expecting to find the angel Gabriel announcing to Mary that she will give birth to a son instead find Luke justifying why he wrote his gospel, and not just to anyone who might read it but specifically "for you, most excellent Theophilus" (1:3).

> *Dedication to Theophilus (1:1-4)*
>
> *(1) Since many have undertaken to set down an orderly account of the events that have been fulfilled among us, (2) just as they were handed on to us by those who from the beginning were eyewitnesses and servants of the word, (3) I too decided, after investigating everything carefully from the very first, to write an orderly account for you, most excellent Theophilus, (4) so that you may know the truth concerning the things about which you have been instructed.*

Who was "most excellent Theophilus," who reappears in the beginning of the Acts of the Apostles (1:1), and why was the book dedicated to him?

In the ancient world, all books were written by hand and then copied by professional scribes or by slaves. In churches, members of the community could have copied small works, for example, the author of Colossians urges his readers to see that his letter was also read in the church of the Laodiceans, thus assuming that there were people in the church at Colossae who could copy it (Col 4:16). But for a book as large as Luke's gospel, to say nothing of Luke and Acts combined, volunteers would not suffice, since very few of them would have the skill or the time to take from their own jobs to do something so demanding and tedious as copying two books by hand.

So how could authors, who were not wealthy, pay to have their works copied? Because of low literacy rates, mass sales were impossible, to say nothing of modern ways to make money, such as television or movie deals. Authors often relied upon patrons, that is, rich people who subsidized the cost of publication. This was the role that Theophilus played, and so Luke acknowledges him in the preface.

Do we know anything about Theophilus besides his name? Luke calls him "most excellent," which suggests he was a nobleman, exactly the type of person who patronized authors, and almost certainly a Gentile, given Luke's primary audience. But is Theophilus even his name? In Greek the name means "beloved of God," so Luke may have meant it in an honorary way. On the other hand, it is known as a proper name; in the late second century the church at Antioch in Syria had a bishop named Theophilus. We cannot answer this question, nor is it important. What really counts is that, thanks to Theophilus, Luke was able to write Luke and Acts.

Luke starts his dedication to Theophilus by noting that "many" other writers produced accounts of what Jesus did. Who were the many others? Luke knew Mark's gospel, but he did not know Matthew's—if he did, they would have harmonized their infancy narratives. Is Luke using some authorial generalization? Were there accounts now lost? We simply do not know.

Luke promises Theophilus an "orderly" account, and he means what he says. As a true literary artist, Luke uses literary devices throughout the gospel and Acts to provide this order for his readers, which lets the readers know that not everything should be taken as absolute history, as we shall soon see, even though the Acts of the Apostles proves that Luke had more interest in history than any other Christian writer of the first or even the second century.

A final point about Theophilus. The modern reader may find this dedication in the introduction to be a distraction, but the ancient reader would have found assurance that Luke was an accomplished writer who had enlisted a literary patron to support his work.

PASTORAL REFLECTION

Christians want to impact the world, but they cannot do so if they do not take part in the world's activities. "Taking part" and "succumbing to" are not equivalent terms. Believers can keep an appropriate distance from inappropriate elements in the modern world, such as rampant commercialism, but, as Luke shows us here, knowing how the world functions is a pre-requisite for influencing the world, and knowing the world allows us to appreciate the many good things that those outside our communities are doing.

> ## The Announcement of the Birth
> ### of John the Baptist (1:5-25)
>
> *(5) In the days of King Herod of Judea, there was a priest named Zechariah, who belonged to the priestly order of Abijah. His wife was a descendant of Aaron, and her name was Elizabeth. (6) Both of them were righteous before God, living blamelessly according to all the commandments and regulations of the Lord. (7) But they had no children, because Elizabeth was barren, and both were getting on in years.*
>
> *(8) Once when he was serving as priest before God and his section was on duty, (9) he was chosen by lot,*

*according to the custom of the priesthood, to enter the
sanctuary of the Lord and offer incense. (10) Now at the
time of the incense offering, the whole assembly of the
people was praying outside. (11) Then there appeared to
him an angel of the Lord, standing at the right side of the
altar of incense. (12) When Zechariah saw him, he was
terrified; and fear overwhelmed him. (13) But the angel
said to him, "Do not be afraid, Zechariah, for your
prayer has been heard. Your wife Elizabeth will bear you
a son, and you will name him John. (14) You will have
joy and gladness, and many will rejoice at his birth, (15)
for he will be great in the sight of the Lord. He must
never drink wine or strong drink; even before his birth
he will be filled with the Holy Spirit. (16) He will turn
many of the people of Israel to the Lord their God. (17)
With the spirit and power of Elijah he will go before him,
to turn the hearts of parents to their children, and the
disobedient to the wisdom of the righteous, to make
ready a people prepared for the Lord." (18) Zechariah
said to the angel, "How will I know that this is so? For I
am an old man, and my wife is getting on in years." (19)
The angel replied, "I am Gabriel. I stand in the presence
of God, and I have been sent to speak to you and to
bring you this good news. (20) But now, because you did
not believe my words, which will be fulfilled in their
time, you will become mute, unable to speak, until the
day these things occur."*

*(21) Meanwhile the people were waiting for Zechariah,
and wondered at his delay in the sanctuary. (22) When
he did come out, he could not speak to them, and they
realized that he had seen a vision in the sanctuary. He
kept motioning to them and remained unable to speak.
(23) When his time of service was ended, he went to his
home.*

> *(24) After those days his wife Elizabeth conceived, and for five months she remained in seclusion. She said, (25) "This is what the Lord has done for me when he looked favorably on me and took away the disgrace I have endured among my people."*

The dedication completed, Luke turns to his two infancy narratives, one about Jesus, of course, but also one about John the Baptist. Recall that both Matthew and Luke wanted to establish that God had acknowledged Jesus as his Son not at his baptism by John but at his birth. But also recall that, in the Acts of the Apostles, Luke is the one who tells us that disciples of John were active twenty years after his death and hundreds of miles from Palestine. Matthew may be content to assert divine recognition at Jesus' birth, but Luke decides to take on the John the Baptist issue directly.

The evangelist tells us that in the days of Herod, two righteous Jews, the priest Zechariah and his wife Elizabeth, "had no children, because Elizabeth was barren, and both were getting on in years" (1:7). Elizabeth considered her inability to have a child a "disgrace I have endured among my people" (1:25). In the ancient, patriarchal world, a woman had one role in life, and that was to have a son so that her husband's family name would continue for another generation. If the couple did not have children, it was always the woman's fault, never her husband's. Since the woman had failed in her main duty to her husband, she suffered disgrace, especially since many ancient Jews considered barrenness a sign of divine disfavor. Nowadays we believe that if a couple cannot have children, it may be a sad occasion for them but certainly not a disgrace. Furthermore, we know the problem could be with the husband or the wife or both. Rather ironically for the ancient view, we also know that biologically the man determines the gender of the child, not the woman, so at no point in history was it the woman's "fault" if she had only daughters. As we shall see, Luke can rise above many of the sexist attitudes of his age, but, as this case shows, not all of them.

Zechariah "was serving as priest before God" in Jerusalem and had entered the sanctuary of the temple (1:8). Suddenly "there appeared to him an angel of the Lord" (1:11). Matthew mentions an angel but provides no name. Luke, however, identifies the angel as Gabriel (1:20), who played a prominent role in ancient Jewish beliefs about angels. Gabriel brings God's messages to the prophet Daniel (Dan 8:16-23), and in Jewish apocryphal literature, that is, those books claiming to be by or about biblical figures but which are not in the Bible, Gabriel plays a prominent role, especially in two books attributed to the Hebrew patriarch Enoch (Gen 1:18-24). These books, called simply First and Second Enoch and dating to the second or first centuries BC, portray Gabriel as a powerful archangel who sits at God's left hand and who, on God's behalf, intervenes in Israelite history.

Gabriel's important status alerts the reader that this is a major announcement from God. It also tells us that although Luke will emphasize the significance of Jesus for all peoples, he never overlooks Jesus' Jewish and Old Testament background.

The angel gives Zechariah the good news that Elizabeth and he will have a son. Gabriel goes on to provide a name for the boy and to predict his greatness: "he will turn many of the people of Israel to the Lord their God" (1:16), and he will "make ready a people prepared for the Lord" (1:17). Since Luke frequently uses the word "Lord" for Jesus (for example, 5:8; 7:6; 10:1; 11:39; 17:5), he here tells the reader that John the Baptist will be preparing for the arrival of Jesus. Even the surprising phrase, "even before his birth he will be filled with the Holy Spirit" (1:15) will fit this pattern of preparation, as we shall soon see. From the opening verses of his gospel, Luke demonstrates John's role in the story of human salvation: he plays an important role but definitely a subordinate one to that of Jesus.

In response to the angelic announcement, Zechariah asks a logical question, "How will I know that this is so? For I am an old man, and my wife is getting on in years" (1:18). The angel replies by identifying himself as Gabriel who stands in God's presence and says that he has brought good news. The Greek verb for "bringing good news" has the same root as the noun *euaggélion*, the word for "gospel." But the priest's question shows his lack of faith in God's power to overcome any obstacle. Gabriel gives him a sign "that this is so," but it is a negative one. Zechariah will be dumb until the boy's birth (1:20).

The priest leaves the sanctuary in such a state that others in the temple know he has seen a vision, but he cannot speak to tell anyone about it. He returns home and has conjugal relations with his wife. Elizabeth conceives and is delighted that her "disgrace" has been removed (1:25).

Readers of the Bible, ancient and modern, would recognize the overall pattern of this narrative. Sarah and Abraham, Rebecca and Isaac, the parents of Samson, and Elkanah and Hannah, the parents of Samuel, all found themselves in the same situation, unable to have a son, and blessed when God removed the barrenness of the wife. Here, however, Luke specifically recalls Abraham and Sarah, because of these OT couples, they alone were elderly (Gen 17).

But Luke also includes parallels to Samuel's birth—Luke 1:15: *"He must never drink wine or strong drink;"* 1 Samuel 1:11: *"He shall drink neither wine nor intoxicants."* And again, Luke 1:24-25: ". . . *his wife Elizabeth conceived, and . . . She said, 'This is what the Lord has done for me when he looked favorably on me . . .'"* 1 Samuel 1:19: *"Elkanah knew his wife Hannah, and the LORD remembered her."*

Luke has thus placed John the Baptist squarely in the history of Israel, has demonstrated that God continues to act in history, and has skillfully set John in an Old Testament environment, which will heighten the differences between Jesus and him. If the age of John's parents is meant to recall Abraham and Sarah, the parents of the Jewish people, then

Luke is here showing his Gentile readers that they form part of a new people through whom God will work.

This is the only gospel passage that says anything about the relatives of Jesus. There are passages that mention relatives (Matt 13:56; Mark 3:31), but only Luke gives us a picture of them—pious Jews wishing for a child, an absence for which even the honor of priesthood could not make up. How happy Elizabeth and Zechariah are to have a son, to know that their family line will continue for another generation.

Relatives can present problems, and certainly many families are unhappy. All problematic and unhappy people disturb us, but difficulties with those who share with us parents or grandparents particularly disturb us. Relatives are irreplaceable, by which I mean, we may make or lose friends and colleagues, but the blood tie exists forever. It is a living link that should not be broken.

Are there relatives from whom we are estranged? Maybe the reason for the estrangement is too strong to overcome, but maybe not. Maybe we should reconsider the situation and try—or at least hope—for reconciliation.

The Announcement of the Birth of Jesus (1:26-38)

(26) In the sixth month the angel Gabriel was sent by God to a town in Galilee called Nazareth, (27) to a virgin engaged to a man whose name was Joseph, of the house of David. The virgin's name was Mary. (28) And he came to her and said, "Greetings, favored one! The Lord is with you." (29) But she was much perplexed by his words and pondered what sort of greeting this might be. (30) The angel said to her, "Do not be afraid, Mary, for you have found favor with God. (31) And now, you will conceive in your womb and bear a son, and you will

> *name him Jesus. (32) He will be great, and will be called*
> *the Son of the Most High, and the Lord God will give to*
> *him the throne of his ancestor David. (33) He will reign*
> *over the house of Jacob forever, and of his kingdom there*
> *will be no end." (34) Mary said to the angel, "How can*
> *this be, since I am a virgin?" (35) The angel said to her,*
> *"The Holy Spirit will come upon you, and the power of*
> *the Most High will overshadow you; therefore the child*
> *to be born will be holy; he will be called Son of God. (36)*
> *And now, your relative Elizabeth in her old age has also*
> *conceived a son; and this is the sixth month for her who*
> *was said to be barren. (37) For nothing will be impos-*
> *sible with God." (38) Then Mary said, "Here am I, the*
> *servant of the Lord; let it be with me according to your*
> *word." Then the angel departed from her.*

Luke now turns to the annunciation of Jesus' birth, and he again relies heavily upon the OT account of the birth of the judge and prophet Samuel (1 Sam 1–2)—Luke 2:6-7: *"While they were there, the time came for her to deliver her child. And she gave birth to her firstborn son"*; 1 Samuel 1:20: *"In due time Hannah conceived and bore a son."* Luke 2:24: *"They offered a sacrifice"*; 1 Samuel 1:21: *"The man Elkanah and all his household went up to offer the* LORD *the yearly sacrifice."* Luke 2:39: *"They returned to Galilee, to their own town of Nazareth"*; 1 Samuel 1:19: *". . . they went back to their house at Ramah."*

This approach provides continuity with the account of John's annunciation and birth and links Jesus to the history of Israel. But the parallel to the birth of Samuel coincides with Luke's introduction of the last living link to the old religion and the first link to the new, Mary.

Matthew may have emphasized Joseph, but Luke's focus falls squarely upon Jesus' mother Mary. What exactly do we know about her?

For starters, her name was Miriam, which became Maria in Greek and Latin, as it is in Italian and Spanish, and became Marie in French and Mary in English.

She lived in Nazareth at the time of the annunciation and was betrothed to a carpenter named Joseph. Several gospel passages show her to be present during Jesus' public career (for example, Mark 3:31-35; John 2:1-11), and John's gospel (19:25) places her under the cross. In the Acts of the Apostles 1:14, Luke tells us she was with Jesus' disciples in the Upper Room after the ascension. Luke says that Elizabeth was her relative (1:36), while John (19:25) adds the detail that she had a sister, about whom nothing is known. But we can augment what the NT tells us by placing Mary within the context of the ancient world.

Up to the nineteenth century, childbirth was the leading cause of death for women, and the ancient world had a high infant mortality rate. People often married as teenagers so that the wife could have many children to guarantee that some would live and, quite frankly, so that the husband would be young enough to marry again if his wife died in childbirth. We can safely presume Mary was about fourteen or fifteen at the time of the annunciation. The *Protoevàngelium of James*, a Christian apocryphal gospel composed around the middle of the second century in Syria, says that Mary was sixteen, but there is no independent way to verify that.

Her parents and Joseph's parents would have arranged the marriage, the common practice in the ancient world and in much of the world even today. For a village girl, marriage to a skilled craftsman would have been considered a good match. As we shall see, Luke shows both Mary and Joseph to have been pious Jews, an important point for their parents to consider when seeking spouses.

Although late medieval and renaissance paintings often portray Mary reading a book when Gabriel appears to her, she would have been illiterate since ancient society saw little reason to educate girls whose purpose in life was, as we just saw, to have sons. Luke tells us that Mary's son could read (4:17), but we cannot say if her husband could.

The *Protoevangelium of James*, claims that Mary's parents were named Joachim and Anna. Since this "gospel" was almost contemporary with the later New Testament writings, is it possible that the names are authentic? Yes, it is possible, but no more than that since the names appear in a miraculous legend about Mary's birth. According to the legend, Joachim and Anna could not have children, but God intervened so that Anna conceived Mary. This account strongly parallels several OT birth narratives, but especially that of the Israelite judge Samuel (1 Sam 1:1–2:10). Samuel's mother was named Hannah, which translates into Greek and Latin as "Anna," the *Protoevangelium*'s name for Mary's mother. These parallels make scholars reluctant to accept the names as historical information. In fact, most of what we know about Mary comes not from various NT or apocryphal books but from the Gospel of Luke, especially its infancy narrative.

Luke clearly has more in mind for Mary than just a historical account. Recall that Matthew's gospel has the man receive the annunciation. Luke has a woman do so, an early sign of a gospel that will emphasize the role of women. Furthermore, in Acts (1:14), Luke tells us that Mary joined the disciples in the Upper Room after Jesus' ascension, so Luke shows Mary as being involved in Jesus' ministry before his birth and after his resurrection, a claim no other Christian could make. The evangelist models Mary as the ideal disciple who faithfully accepts God's wishes for her at the annunciation, who keeps her faith during Jesus' ministry, and who, in effect, becomes one of the first Christians after his resurrection. For Luke, Mary personally makes the transition from Judaism to Christianity. This discipleship theme will appear with some frequency in Luke's infancy narrative.

Luke tells us that "in the sixth month" of Elizabeth's pregnancy, "the angel Gabriel was sent by God to a town in

Galilee called Nazareth" (1:26). As we saw in the last chapter, Matthew and Luke disagree on where Mary and Joseph lived before Jesus' birth. Luke says that they were in Nazareth, while Matthew (2:23) says that, fearful of returning to Judea, they went to Nazareth after their return from Egypt. Both evangelists agree that Jesus grew up in that town.

The annunciation to Mary appears in some detail in Luke (1:26-38), in contrast to Matthew's bare, two-verse (1:20-21) account of the annunciation to Joseph, and Luke's account fits his Christology of Jesus as the universal savior since a woman becomes the first witness to the Incarnation just as women will be the first witnesses of the resurrection in all four gospel accounts. Like Matthew, Luke records that Mary was a virgin, proof that both drew upon a common early Christian tradition. Luke does not include Matthew's dramatic scene of Joseph's wishing to put her away quietly, nor does Luke cite Isaiah. Her virginity causes Mary to ask how her pregnancy might occur; the angel responds; and Mary, "the handmaiden" and faithful disciple, accepts God's call to her.

For Luke, Mary's virginity plays an important role in his comparison of John the Baptist and Jesus. Comparison of the annunciation accounts shows us Luke the literary artist at work. Even casual readers notice some similarities between the annunciation to Zechariah about John and to Mary about Jesus, for example, both of them are afraid but the angel tells them not to be afraid (1:12-13, 29-30), but these similarities are not casual. Luke has used a device called a step-parallel, that is, he parallels the two annunciations, but he puts the one to Mary on a step higher than the one to Zechariah in terms of the children's future.

	Birth of John	*Birth of Jesus*
Angel	Gabriel	Gabriel
Recipient	Zechariah (man)	Mary (woman)
Child	John	Jesus
Future	Filled with Holy Spirit Bring Israelites to God Make people ready for the Lord	Son of the Most High Occupy throne of David Kingdom without end
Obstacle	Age of parents	Mary's virginity
Sign	Zechariah struck dumb	Elizabeth's pregnancy

Luke is not subtle. John's greatness goes unquestioned, but it cannot match that of Jesus. John will be filled with the Holy Spirit, but the spirit of God also came upon Othoniel (Judg 3:9-10), Saul (1 Sam 11:16), and Zechariah the priest (2 Chr 24:20), as well as other OT figures. Jesus, by contrast, is the Son of the Most High. John will bring the Israelites to God, but Jesus will occupy David's throne, a Messianic image. John will prepare the way of "the Lord," a familiar Lukan title for Jesus, making it clear what John's role would be, a role that would fade in time, while Jesus would reign without end.

The "step up" goes beyond the predictions. As the Old Testament witnessed, God overcame a woman's barrenness several times, but nowhere in the OT does a virgin conceive. The greater miracle fits the greater child, while simultaneously allowing Luke to show that the Old Testament has no figure comparable to Jesus. This greater miracle also befits Jesus' mother, an important figure in Luke's gospel.

Even the two signs play a role. Zechariah received a negative sign, a physical impairment, while Mary received a positive one, the pregnancy of her relative Elizabeth.

The modern believer, often anxious for history, may be a bit uncomfortable with the obvious literary devices at work here, but ancient readers would have appreciated Luke's skill. As we shall see, Luke liked this annunciation pattern so much that he used it a third time.

He also related the annunciation to Jesus' public career. The Holy Spirit appears more frequently in Luke's gospel than in any other and also appears prominently in the Acts of the Apostles, most notably at Pentecost but in many other passages as well. Matthew has the angel tell Joseph that the child Mary carries is "from the Holy Spirit" (1:20), but Luke dramatically says that "the Holy Spirit will come upon you, and the power of the Most High will overshadow you" (1:35). "Overshadow" is an unusual verb, but it has an OT base. It appears in Exodus 40:35 and Numbers 9:18, 22, to describe the cloud of God's glory overshadowing the Tabernacle, and also in Exodus 25:20 and 1 Chronicles 28:18 to describe the winged cherubim overshadowing the Ark of the Covenant; such events are *theophanies*, manifestations of the divine. Luke uses "overshadow" again at the Transfiguration (9:34-35) when the cloud (recalling the OT theophanies) from which the voice speaks overshadows the three disciples (James, John, Peter) and manifests the presence of God to them, saying, "This is my Son, my Chosen." Luke brilliantly portrays the divine origins of Jesus by an angelic announcement at his conception and a heavenly voice from the cloud during his ministry.

PASTORAL REFLECTION

Mary has long been an object of veneration for many Christians, especially in the Orthodox and Roman Catholic churches, but much of that veneration is non-scriptural, that is, it does not portray the humble, hardworking, peasant woman of the gospel. Let me emphasize that people can venerate Mary in many ways; my concern is that some veneration simply overlooks the biblical Mary.

For example, in the Middle Ages people referred to her as *Notre Dame*, literally "Our Lady," a name on many medieval churches. Today the word "lady" means a polite, well-mannered woman, a complimentary title for any woman, but in the Middle Ages a "lady" was a noblewoman, an aristocrat, someone who had little contact with or interest in peasants like Mary. Eventually Mary became venerated as *Regina* or Queen, a woman whose royal stature separated her completely from the people. Medieval devotion did something else to Mary. It robbed her of her Jewishness. Works of art portrayed a tall, beautiful, pale-skinned Nordic woman with golden hair, but never a sunburned Near Eastern woman with calluses on her hands from all the hard work she did. Partly this imagery reflected idealization of a beloved religious figure, partly it reflected the prevalent medieval anti-Semitism, which, so tragically and ironically, would deny both Jesus and his mother their birthright.

Clearly we must respect the earlier generations of Christians, who produced magnificent Marian art and architecture and sustained Marian devotion for centuries, but in a book focused on the Bible, let us image Mary in a scriptural way. Let us see her first as the Jew that she was and was proud to be, a full-blooded member of God's Chosen People. Let us see her as a Jewish peasant woman, hard-working, worried about money problems, about domestic issues, and about her oppressed people.

Let us see her as a mother, but let us also see her as a wife. So much Marian devotion simply ignores Joseph, yet they lived together for decades in what was surely a happy married life. Instead of artwork showing a European-looking queen, why not represent Mary and Joseph embracing or holding hands or just walking together? Why not show them enjoying one another's company? We should not be reluctant to image Mary as the gospels do—as Joseph's wife.

Mary Visits Elizabeth (1:39-45)

(39) In those days Mary set out and went with haste to a Judean town in the hill country, (40) where she entered the house of Zechariah and greeted Elizabeth. (41) When Elizabeth heard Mary's greeting, the child leaped in her womb. And Elizabeth was filled with the Holy Spirit (42) and exclaimed with a loud cry, "Blessed are you among women, and blessed is the fruit of your womb. (43) And why has this happened to me, that the mother of my Lord comes to me? (44) For as soon as I heard the sound of your greeting, the child in my womb leaped for joy. (45) And blessed is she who believed that there would be a fulfillment of what was spoken to her by the Lord."

Having just been informed by an angel that she will bear the Savior, Mary does not succumb to pride at this astonishing honor, but rather this humble woman and model disciple decides to perform a simple act of charity. Concerned about the difficulties an elderly woman would encounter with a pregnancy, she visits Elizabeth. Mary greets her relative, and "when Elizabeth heard Mary's greeting, the child leaped in her womb" (1:41), that is, John acknowledges the presence of Jesus, which in turn fulfills part of Gabriel's prediction to Zechariah (1:15) that John would be filled with the Holy Spirit even before his birth. The Israelite prophets were filled with the Holy Spirit as is the unborn John when he acknowledges the unborn Jesus.

In addition to that, Elizabeth says to Mary, "blessed are you among women" and also blessed is "the fruit of your womb" (1:42). She identifies Mary as "the mother of my Lord," thus using the title Luke used of Jesus and recalling the annunciation to Zechariah that John would prepare the way of the Lord. Luke makes his point forcefully—both the unborn John the Baptist and his own mother recognize that Jesus is the

Lord. Elizabeth also calls Mary blessed because she believed what the angel said (1:45), keeping with Luke's emphasis on Mary as the model disciple.

PASTORAL REFLECTION

Here Luke shows Mary performing an essential element of Jewish piety, caring for an older relative. To be sure, Luke's focus is on showing the superiority of Jesus to John, but he simultaneously shows a pregnant woman who worries not about how tired she might become from a journey but rather about helping someone else. Luke emphasizes Elizabeth's spiritual joy, but we can also imagine her personal joy at seeing her young relative. The modern cult of youth often relegates the elderly off to the side, but the ancient world prized the elderly—not, as is often thought, for their supposed wisdom but because they were family, a link to previous and unknown generations and progenitors of generations to come. And, very often, people simply in need of assistance, which we, like Mary, should provide.

> ### The Magnificat (1:46-56)
>
> (46) And Mary said,
>> "My soul magnifies the Lord,
> (47)   and my spirit rejoices in God my Savior,
> (48) for he has looked with favor on the lowliness of his
>>> servant.
>> Surely, from now on all generations will call me
>>> blessed;
> (49) for the Mighty One has done great things for me,
>> and holy is his name.
> (50) His mercy is for those who fear him
>> from generation to generation.
> (51) He has shown strength with his arm;
>> he has scattered the proud in the thoughts
>>> of their hearts.

> (52) He has brought down the powerful from their
> thrones,
>   and lifted up the lowly;
> (53) he has filled the hungry with good things,
>   and sent the rich away empty.
> (54) He has helped his servant Israel,
>   in remembrance of his mercy,
> (55) according to the promise he made to our ancestors,
>   to Abraham and to his descendants forever."
>
> (56) And Mary remained with her about three months
> and then returned to her home.

Luke turns to another central point of his gospel, Jesus' concern for the outcast, the marginalized, and the oppressed. He does this by Mary's recitation of a famous versified prayer, the *Magnificat*, which he composed himself but almost certainly incorporated some existing Christian prayers within it.

Two questions arise immediately: How can scholars be sure that Luke wrote this prayer? And why is it called by a Latin title?

Recall that ancient writers could insert speeches in the mouths of their characters, so here Luke acts like an ancient writer. But could not the *Magnificat* have been uttered by Mary and then translated by Luke? Not really. The versification depends upon Greek poetic metres and so cannot be a translation. This work came from a skilled Greek writer, not an illiterate teenage girl speaking Aramaic whose words were remembered and faithfully recited for eight decades before being translated into Greek by Luke. Once again, *we* may worry about the historicity of every event in the gospel, but first-century Christians would have valued Luke's literary artistry. Yet the evangelist may not have created this work completely. The *Magnificat* has similarities to the prayer of Hannah in 1 Samuel 2:1-10 and the prophet Jonah's prayer in Jonah 2:2-9. Luke may also have drawn from existing Jewish traditions known and used among the earliest Christians.

As for the title, in the Middle Ages few Western European Christians had any knowledge of Greek, and so they relied upon Latin translations of the Bible. In Latin the first words of this prayer, "My soul magnifies the Lord," would be *Magnificat anima mea Dominum*. The prayer came to be known by the first word of the Latin version; the term is still used, and this will be true of three other passages in Luke's infancy narrative (*Benedictus*, *Gloria*, and *Nunc Dimittis*).

The *Magnificat* (1:46-55) contains many Lukan themes. The Lord "has looked with favor on the lowliness of his servant" Mary, that is, God chose to work the world's salvation through a woman. In doing so, he elevated her so that "from now on all generations will call me blessed" (1:48). God "has scattered the proud . . . he has brought down the powerful from their thrones, and lifted up the lowly; he has filled the hungry with good things, and sent the rich away empty" (1:51-53). The people whom the worldly admire—the rich and powerful—have been turned away by God who cares for the hungry and the lowly, the same themes Luke will return to in his version of the beatitudes and indeed throughout much of the gospel.

The *Magnificat* finishes with Luke's careful reminder that the savior of all people has emerged from the history of Israel. God "has helped his servant Israel . . . according to the promise he made to our ancestors. . . ." (1:54-55).

We also note one other intriguing point. Elizabeth's words to Mary and her response constitute the only conversation between two women without a man present in the entire New Testament.

Luke ends his account of Mary's visit by saying that she returned home after a three-month stay with Elizabeth.

PASTORAL REFLECTION

A pastoral reflection on the *Magnificat* seems superfluous, since the pastoral application is so obvious. Luke here offers an assurance to all those who suffer, who have been oppressed, who feel that the system works against them, that someone always cares.

But if God cares so much, why does anyone continue to suffer? No believer has an answer. Another biblical book, Job, concludes that innocent suffering must remain a mystery and all that sufferers can do is trust that God has not forgotten them.

But if we cannot answer why God seems absent, we do not have to wonder why we seem absent. God's reasons are unfathomable, but ours are not. Let us all ask ourselves how we are living up to Mary's call in the *Magnificat*.

The Birth of John the Baptist (1:57-66)

(57) Now the time came for Elizabeth to give birth, and she bore a son. (58) Her neighbors and relatives heard that the Lord had shown his great mercy to her, and they rejoiced with her.

(59) On the eighth day they came to circumcise the child, and they were going to name him Zechariah after his father. (60) But his mother said, "No; he is to be called John." (61) They said to her, "None of your relatives has this name." (62) Then they began motioning to his father to find out what name he wanted to give him. (63) He asked for a writing tablet and wrote, "His name is John." And all of them were amazed. (64) Immediately his mouth was opened and his tongue freed, and he began to speak, praising God. (65) Fear came over all their neighbors, and all these things were talked about throughout the entire hill country of Judea. (66) All who heard them pondered them and said, "What then will this child become?" For, indeed, the hand of the Lord was with him.

Now Luke finishes the story of John's birth, saying simply that "the time came for Elizabeth to give birth, and she bore a son." The drama begins on the eighth day, the day of circumcision, when the parents will name the child. Relatives want to call him Zechariah after his father, and, as to be expected, they do not listen to the woman when Elizabeth insists on the name John. They turn to Zechariah to see what the man wants, and he writes on a tablet, "His name is John," to the amazement of the relatives. The little episode has a curious element. When the relatives want to know what Zechariah thinks, "they began motioning . . . to find out what name he wanted to give him" (1:62). But why? Motioning implies that Zechariah was deaf as well as dumb, thus adding an impairment to the one imposed upon Zechariah by the angel Gabriel (1:20). This is a rare slipup for the otherwise careful evangelist.

As the angel said, when John was named, Zechariah regained his power of speech, a miracle which both frightened and impressed all who saw it. But more was at stake than a fulfillment of Gabriel's words. God has a task for Zechariah to carry out, and he must speak to do it. In a foreshadowing of Mary's reaction to Jesus' birth (2:19), the Jews who hear of the events surrounding John's birth "pondered them and said, 'What then will this child become?'" (1:66). Inspired by the Holy Spirit, Zechariah will answer the question with a prophecy about his newborn son (1:67-79).

PASTORAL REFLECTION

What will any child become? It is a good question, and the answer will not be known for decades. Many people sink to low levels in life, such as drug dealing and theft, and we always wonder how that happened. Drug dealers and thieves used to be the hopes of their parents, who thought that their children would enjoy success in business or the professions, and that they would make the world a better place.

Children are our ultimate legacy to the world. They enter the world in total innocence, and what they become depends so much on their parents, siblings, and those around them. But it also depends upon the society in which they will grow up. Do we offer them a world in which their better inclinations will be welcomed, or do we offer them a world in which violence, dishonesty, and avarice are considered necessary parts of life? Do we have leaders who think negotiation and reconciliation are signs of weakness? Do we have an attitude that presumes that everyone cheats, so we had better too? Do our values tell children that people are measured more by what they own than by whom they help?

When Elizabeth's and Zechariah's friends wondered what the child would become, did they think that they would have a hand in it? All of us, parents or not, owe children a better world.

The Benedictus (1:67-80)

(67) Then his father Zechariah was filled with the Holy
Spirit and spoke this prophecy:
(68) "Blessed be the Lord God of Israel,
  for he has looked favorably on his people and
  redeemed them.
(69) He has raised up a mighty savior for us
  in the house of his servant David,
(70) as he spoke through the mouth of his holy prophets
  from of old,
(71) that we would be saved from our enemies and
  from the hand of all who hate us.
(72) Thus he has shown the mercy promised to our
  ancestors,
  and has remembered his holy covenant,

(73) the oath that he swore to our ancestor Abraham,
　　to grant us (74) that we, being rescued from the
　　　hands of our enemies,
　　might serve him without fear, (75) in holiness
　　　and righteousness
　　　before him all our days.
(76) And you, child, will be called the prophet of the
　　　Most High;
　　for you will go before the Lord to prepare his ways,
(77) to give knowledge of salvation to his people
　　by the forgiveness of their sins.
(78) By the tender mercy of our God,
　　the dawn from on high will break upon us,
(79) to give light to those who sit in darkness and in the
　　　shadow of death,
　　to guide our feet into the way to peace."

*(80) The child grew and became strong in spirit, and he
was in the wilderness until the day he appeared publicly
to Israel.*

The prophecy begins "Blessed be the Lord God of Israel,"
which in Latin reads *Benedictus Dominus Deus Israhel*. Medieval Christians thus called this the *Benedictus*, and modern
scholars still use the name. The prophecy runs for twelve
verses, eight of which recount what God did for his people
Israel, citing both David and Abraham, and claiming fulfillment of ancient prophecies. But, speaking not of John, Zechariah says "[God] has raised up a mighty savior for us in the
house of his servant David" (1:69), recalling Gabriel's words
to Mary that God will give her son "the throne of his ancestor
David" (1:32). Again we see Luke aligning his infancy narrative with God's work in the history of Israel. Luke also looks
forward to the Acts of the Apostles where he will recount how
God works in the history of his new people.

The last verses focus on John's future as Zechariah addresses his infant son. Specifically, "you, child, will be called the prophet of the Most High; for you will go before the Lord to prepare his ways" (1:76). John's mother had called Jesus "Lord," so Luke makes it clear: John will prepare the way for Jesus. Forceful in this regard, Luke wrote more subtly on another theme, that the work of John brought to a conclusion the history of Israel as recounted in the Old Testament. That history pointed to Jesus from his earliest ancestor Abraham right down to his relative John, son of Abraham and Sarah figures.

Luke's infancy narrative bids farewell to John as we learn "the child grew and became strong in spirit, and he was in the wilderness until the day he appeared publicly to Israel" (1:80). Luke does not explain what he meant by "he was in the wilderness until the day he appeared." Did John go to the wilderness before he was an adult? Did his parents entrust him to the Jews at the desert settlement of Qumran on the Dead Sea, the community that produced the Dead Sea Scrolls? There is no way to tell. All we can say is that Luke provides a transition to John's presence in the wilderness when he reappears as an adult in chapter 3. Luke will do the same for Jesus at the end of chapter 2, finishing an account of childhood and going immediately to his public career.

PASTORAL REFLECTION

Luke intends this passage to reinforce his picture of John as Jesus' forerunner, and so he has Zechariah making elaborate statements about his son's future. But if we get away from the formal, dramatic language, we can wonder what Zechariah—and Elizabeth, who says nothing—must have thought about John's calling. The Israelite prophets rarely led happy lives. Hosea married an unfaithful wife; Jeremiah was loathed by the people and actually imprisoned for a while; Ezekiel was exiled to Babylon with other leading Jews; in Jewish tradition, Isaiah was murdered. John's parents could hardly have expected that he would lead a joyful life, and how sad that must have been for them, looking at a beautiful newborn child and already having to fear for his future.

When we recall that John prepared the way of the Lord, we realize that he personally never followed Jesus, that is, he was never a Christian. Here we see yet one more Jew, one more person not part of the Christian community, doing God's work. Let us let John still prepare the way of the Lord by helping to remember how God works through all people and how much we draw from their selfless service.

With the end of chapter 1, Elizabeth and Zechariah pass from the scene, and Luke will make no reference to John's being a relative of Jesus in the account of the public ministry, but the account of John and his parents has fulfilled a major concern of Luke by establishing the superiority of Jesus' mission and person to those of John, right from their conceptions.

Chapter 1 has also introduced Mary in two prominent passages, the annunciation and the visitation, establishing her importance for his infancy narrative and for other parts of his gospel and even Acts. Chapter 2 now turns to Mary, her husband, and her infant son.

Chapter 2

Many Christian scholars believe that chapters 1 and 2 were once individual episodes that Luke brought together. To quote an ecumenical study group led by Raymond E. Brown and Karl Donfried, ". . . no single fact of chap. 1 is presupposed by chap. 2. For instance, in 2:4 the reader is again told that Jesus was of the house of David, and in 2:5 Mary is reintroduced as the betrothed of Joseph, as if those facts had not been mentioned in 1:27. . . . Joseph, who was only named in chap. 1, emerges almost as an equal partner with Mary in the narrative of chap. 2." To this we can add that chapter 2 does not mention Elizabeth, Zechariah, or their son. But whatever the source material might have been, the finished narrative belongs to Luke.

The Birth of Jesus (2:1-7)

(1) In those days a decree went out from Emperor [Caesar] Augustus that all the world should be registered. (2) This was the first registration and was taken while Quirinius was governor of Syria. (3) All went to their own towns to be registered. (4) Joseph also went from the town of Nazareth in Galilee to Judea, to the city of David called Bethlehem, because he was descended from the house and family of David. (5) He went to be registered with Mary, to whom he was engaged and who was expecting a child. (6) While they were there, the time came for her to deliver her child. (7) And she gave birth to her firstborn son and wrapped him in bands of cloth [swaddling clothes], and laid him in a manger, because there was no place for them in the inn.

Why does Luke start the chapter with this census announcement?

First, he provides a historical setting. He has told us these events occurred when Herod was king of Judea (1:5), now he brings in Caesar Augustus who reigned from 31 BC to AD 14, as well as Quirinius the governor of Syria (2:2), the large Roman province which included Judea. Luke repeats this approach at the beginning of Jesus' public ministry (3:1-2).

Second, Augustus had great symbolic value for Luke. Through a shrewd combination of political skills and military planning, Augustus defeated Mark Antony and Cleopatra in 31 BC and awed the Roman senate into allowing him to rule on his own. He took the name Caesar (found in many translations of this passage) from his adoptive father, Julius Caesar, and the name came to be the official title for the emperor. Most Romans welcomed Augustus' rule because he put an end to two decades of civil war and ushered in an era of peace. Battles with barbarian tribes continued on the frontiers, but Augustus could legitimately claim to be the prince of peace. Luke's reader would know all this, and thus they would realize that the angelic announcement of Jesus' birth and of peace on earth (2:14) contrasted the enforced harmony of Augustus with the divinely-given peace ushered in by Jesus.

Third, Augustus ruled from imperial Rome, a far cry from lowly Bethlehem, but, as always, we must recall that Luke also wrote the Acts of the Apostles, which closes with his hero, the Apostle Paul, preaching the faith in Rome (Acts 28). The birth of Jesus would have consequences not just for his own people but for the entire Roman world and even beyond.

Fourth, Luke obviously enjoys contrasting the great emperor with the humble baby. By earthly standards, there is no contest—Augustus is the greater figure. But Augustus had passed into history when Luke wrote, while the resurrected, living Christ enjoys a kingdom without end (1:33).

As we saw, Luke uses the census to explain how Jesus' parents lived in Nazareth yet he was born in Bethlehem. But the census explanation presents serious problems. Publius Sulpicius Quirinius became governor of Syria in AD 6, ten years after the death of Herod and thus at least ten years after Jesus' birth. Possibly Luke had the wrong governor; equally possibly he got the date of the census wrong. Either way, this passage cannot be totally correct historically. But Luke does score one point here. He wrote after Nero's persecution of the Roman Christians in AD 64, and he knew that the Romans questioned the Christians' loyalty. Here he shows Jesus' parents obeying Roman law, just as their son would do.

Mary and Joseph travel to Bethlehem because Joseph was "from the house and family of David" (2:4), and David's father Jesse had lived in Bethlehem (1 Sam 17:12). When they get to the town, Mary can sense the imminent birth.

Unable to find lodgings, Joseph and Mary lay the baby in a manger, "because there was no place for them in the inn" (2:7). A manger is a trough that was used for animal feed, and thus the source of the traditional image of Jesus being laid upon hay and straw. Luke does not say where Mary and Joseph stayed, but since a manger would have been in a barn, he implies that they would have slept there. Note also that Luke says simply "no place" and does not even hint at the traditional image of the cruel innkeeper heartlessly refusing them a room. Such an image may be more dramatic, but it is simply a later legend. But, temporarily at least, the Holy Family is homeless, thus aligning them with the deprived, impoverished people to whom Jesus would preach.

And what exactly are these "bands of cloth" which many translations call by the term "swaddling clothes" (2:7)? This means that Mary wrapped strips of cloth around Jesus, following a Palestinian custom and belief that if the newborn child's arms and legs were kept straight at her or his side, the child would have straight limbs later in life. Early Christian and medieval art routinely show the baby Jesus all bundled up, almost like a mummy.

In just seven short verses, Luke has recounted Jesus' birth. Now he turns to the important events that occurred subsequent to it.

PASTORAL REFLECTION

This passage has similar pastoral elements to previous Lukan ones. An emperor in faraway Rome wants a census, and he imperially commands all the men and, presumably, unmarried adult women to register for the census in the towns in which they were born. For many people this would have meant a short walk down the street, but for many others, like Joseph, it involved a not inconsiderable trip. Did the emperor care? Of course not. Disrupting people's lives for his own purpose would mean nothing to him. Poor people were at his disposal, a situation we see today in many parts of the world.

Many of the world's people have few if any rights, and even if Luke's census presents some historical problems, the image he creates rings true. Why don't people in democracies do more to change this situation? Partly, of course, we do not have the power; partly, we do not have the will when the current dictator aids our political goals or controls some valuable natural resource, such as oil. But partly it is our own upbringing. Living in a democracy, we cannot understand a government, a society, a religious institution, that does not care about what people think or does not extend any rights to them.

I started this book by trying to explain the different worldview the ancients had compared to ours and how we must bridge that gap to understand the Scriptures. We also have to overcome our own worldview to make sense of the deprivation suffered by many today who, like Mary and Joseph, are just pawns in political power plays.

The Shepherds and the Angels (2:8-20)

(8) In that region there were shepherds living in the fields, keeping watch over their flock by night. (9) Then an angel of the Lord stood before them, and the glory of the Lord shone around them, and they were terrified. (10) But the angel said to them, "Do not be afraid; for see—I am bringing you good news of great joy for all the people: (11) to you is born this day in the city of David a Savior, who is the Messiah, the Lord. (12) This will be a sign for you: you will find a child wrapped in bands of cloth and lying in a manger." (13) And suddenly there was with the angel a multitude of the heavenly host, praising God and saying, (14) "Glory to God in the highest heaven, and on earth peace among those whom he favors!"

(15) When the angels had left them and gone into heaven, the shepherds said to one another, "Let us go now to Bethlehem and see this thing that has taken place, which the Lord has made known to us." (16) So

> *they went with haste and found Mary and Joseph, and the child lying in the manger. (17) When they saw this, they made known what had been told them about this child; (18) and all who heard it were amazed at what the shepherds told them. (19) But Mary treasured all these words and pondered them in her heart. (20) The shepherds returned, glorifying and praising God for all they had heard and seen, as it had been told them.*

Luke accentuates the shepherds because they were poor, dirty, smelled of animal odors, and did work that others shunned. They were "the lowly" whom the *Magnificat* promised God would lift up (1:52). They also paralleled the humble Mary because they too received an angelic annunciation. Luke follows the same pattern as in chapter 1. An angel (here not identified as Gabriel) appears to the shepherds; they are afraid; the angel tells them not to fear, makes an announcement of "great joy" (2:10) about the birth of a child (here in the past, not future), and gives the child's name (Christ the Lord) and a sign (a baby wrapped in swaddling clothes). Note Luke's language in verse 2:11: "*to you is born* this day . . . ," thus keeping the parental image of the announcements to Zechariah and Mary.

"And suddenly there was with the angel a multitude of the heavenly host, praising God and saying, 'Glory to God in the highest heaven, and on earth peace among those whom he favors'" (2:13-14). What happened to the familiar "and on earth peace to men of good will"? That famous and now traditional phrase is actually an English translation of a Latin translation, *et in terra pax hominibus bonae voluntatis*. The verse simply does not say that in the Greek. The Latin translation of the angelic praise came to be known as the *Gloria* and has often been put to music by great composers such as Vivaldi, Haydn, and Mozart. It has also been repeated in numberless accounts of the Nativity.

Nor should we let this minor concern prevent us from seeing Luke's central point: the celestial choir provides a heavenly witness to Jesus' birth that parallels the earthly witnesses.

The angels depart, and the shepherds go to Bethlehem where they find the Holy Family (2:16). Next comes a strange passage. "When they [the shepherds] saw this [the child in the manger], they made known what had been told them about this child; and all who heard it were amazed at what the shepherds told them" (2:17-18). Yet Luke never tells us who "all who heard it" were, nor why their amazement did not spread throughout the region and attract curious crowds. Perhaps we should understand these people symbolically as future believers "who hear the word of God and obey it" (Luke 11:28). The shepherds now depart and disappear into history.

But the shepherds' account of their angelic vision has a special effect on one person: "Mary treasured all these words and pondered them in her heart" (2:19). Presumably Joseph also heard the same words, but, as usual, Luke focuses on the woman.

PASTORAL REFLECTION

Again we have a classic Lukan theme—the divine message going to the poor—that does not seem to need much help from me. But there may be another theme to consider besides the poverty of the shepherds, namely that Luke uses the angels to demonstrate that what happened on earth had consequences in heaven.

That is a difficult concept, that what we do can affect spiritual beings, but think of it this way. God loves us. When you love someone, you become vulnerable to being hurt by that person—sometimes an unkind word, sometimes a thoughtless act, sometimes genuine betrayal. We cannot pretend we are indifferent to what those who love us do, and why should we think that God is? We too often think of God as impersonal, the creator of heaven and earth who cannot possibly be personally affected by what we lowly humans do. But if we believe that he loves us, then we know that our wrong actions truly hurt him, not in the sense that God is damaged, but in the sense that he suffers disappointment. But, like all those who love us, he forgives the person who hurts him and tries to help that person do better.

> ### *Jesus is Named and Presented in the Temple (2:21-24)*
>
> *(21) After eight days had passed, it was time to circumcise the child; and he was called Jesus, the name given by the angel before he was conceived in the womb.*
>
> *(22) When the time came for their purification according to the law of Moses, they brought him up to Jerusalem to present him to the Lord (23) (as it is written in the law of the Lord, "Every firstborn male shall be designated as holy to the Lord"), (24) and they offered a sacrifice according to what is stated in the law of the Lord, "a pair of turtledoves or two young pigeons."*

"After eight days had passed, it was time to circumcise the child" (2:21), which Mary and Joseph do. Luke has shown Jesus' parents obeying Roman law by registering with the census, and now he shows them obeying the Jewish law as well. Furthermore, they name the boy Jesus, thus obeying God's word as transmitted by Gabriel. Writing in the 80s and aware of Roman suspicions of the Christians, Luke demonstrates a tradition of obedience on the part of Jesus' parents and, by implication, of him and his disciples as well.

To further this point, Luke next shows Mary and Joseph obeying another aspect of the Jewish Law. They go to the Jerusalem Temple "when the time came for *their* purification" (2:22). The Gentile evangelist here shows his unfamiliarity with Jewish law. Only Mary, the woman, needs to be purified from the uncleanness of the birth. The book of Leviticus (12:2-8) specified the time required for purification as forty days (which is why Candlemas, the British feast commemorating this event, falls on February 2). They also present their son in the temple and make a sacrifice.

This brief passage does not offer much for reflection, especially with its attitude toward women (Mary but not Joseph is unclean), but it can make us think about the importance of religious institutions. For many people institutions by their very nature prevent true religiosity since they are often concerned with status, authority, and the petty details that work against the spiritual life. But we never forget how institutions have kept religions alive, even in difficult periods, such as the Russian Orthodox Church during Communist rule in the Soviet Union. Institutions provide permanence and continuity, and institutions have the historical memory that individuals do not. The Holy Family respected the institutions of their religion, but Jesus was willing to challenge institutions when they strayed, putting their own concerns ahead of those of the people whom they should serve.

The Nunc Dimittis (2:25-35)

(25) Now there was a man in Jerusalem whose name was Simeon; this man was righteous and devout, looking forward to the consolation of Israel, and the Holy Spirit rested on him. (26) It had been revealed to him by the Holy Spirit that he would not see death before he had seen the Lord's Messiah. (27) Guided by the Spirit, Simeon came into the temple; and when the parents brought in the child Jesus, to do for him what was customary under the law, (28) Simeon took him in his arms and praised God, saying,

(29) "Master, now you are dismissing your servant in
    peace,
      according to your word;

> *(30) for my eyes have seen your salvation,*
> *(31)   which you prepared in the presence of all peoples,*
> *(32) a light for revelation to the Gentiles*
>   *and for glory to your people Israel."*
>
> *(33) And the child's father and mother were amazed at*
> *what was being said about him. (34) Then Simeon*
> *blessed them and said to his mother Mary, "This child is*
> *destined for the falling and the rising of many in Israel,*
> *and to be a sign that will be opposed (35) so that the*
> *inner thoughts of many will be revealed—and a sword*
> *will pierce your own soul too."*

A new figure enters the story, a "righteous and devout" man (2:25) named Simeon. "It had been revealed to him by the Holy Spirit that he would not see death before he had seen the Lord's Messiah. Guided by the Spirit, Simeon came into the temple" (2:26-27). The Spirit animated the Old Testament prophets, inspired Elizabeth (1:41), and filled John the Baptist in the womb (1:15), so Luke's readers will understand that Simeon's message to Jesus' parents came directly from God. In a touching passage, Simeon takes the infant Christ into his arms before he prophesies (2:29-32). His prophecy is known as the *Nunc Dimittis* ("you are now dismissing"), once again from a medieval Latin translation.

The words of Simeon's prophecy would hardly have surprised Luke's readers. Speaking to God, Simeon refers to the infant boy as "your salvation, which you have prepared in the presence of all peoples, a light for revelation to the Gentiles and for glory to your people Israel." Luke invokes a familiar theme: salvation for all, Gentiles and Jews. The church may be becoming increasingly Gentile, but God will never abandon his chosen people. Note also that Luke has a Jewish prophet call Jesus "a light for revelation to the Gentiles" (2:32).

Next comes a puzzling verse, if taken literally: "And the child's father and mother were amazed at what was being said about him" (2:33). But why? After an angelic annunciation, a virginal conception, and angels in the sky, they could hardly have been surprised by a prophecy. As noted earlier, most scholars believe that chapter 2 partly consists of previously independent elements that Luke formed into a narrative. Possibly the tradition about Simeon originally made no reference to earlier miraculous events, and Luke did not integrate the Simeon account seamlessly into the larger narrative. If so, that would explain why, at this point in the narrative, Mary and Joseph are amazed.

Simeon's prophecy now turns ominous: the child is "to be a sign that will be opposed" (2:34), and Mary will not escape sadness: "a sword will pierce your own soul too" (2:35). The prophecy to Mary has caused confusion over the centuries because many Christians assumed it applied to her presence under the cross at her son's death. But that cannot be because Luke, who records the prophecy, does not place Mary under the cross; that appears only in John's gospel (19:25-27), which had not yet been written. Luke would not have included a foreshadowing that he then failed to fulfill in his gospel. Since his passion narrative cannot fulfill the prophecy, we must look elsewhere, most logically in the infancy narrative. In fact, the fulfillment will occur when Mary and Joseph take the twelve-year-old Jesus to the temple (2:41-51). But first Luke puts in another passage.

PASTORAL REFLECTION

Contrary to some popular belief, Simeon does not ask God to let him die—why would he want to do that when he just discovered such joy? In fact, Luke does not even tell us that Simeon was old, only that the Holy Spirit had promised him that he would not experience death before seeing the Messiah. The emphasis here falls not upon Simeon's relief that his search is over but rather upon how God fulfilled his promise to Simeon in the child Jesus. So often God seems far away; even Jesus asked "My God, my God, why have you forsaken me?" Surely over the years Simeon must have wondered if the promise would come true.

At this point many people might say that if we wait long enough, we will feel the divine presence, but we know that is not true. In the Third World there are people who are born hungry and who die hungry. Have they ever felt the divine presence? We believe that God is indeed there with them; but how much better, they might believe, if God manifests his presence with food and drink. Yet God does not do that. Why not? This is and must remain one of the great mysteries of the faith—a good God who is always there but is so often unknown to us. The story of Simeon can only remind us that God never deserts us, but waiting in faith for him can be a trial.

Anna and the Return to Nazareth (2:36-40)

(36) There was also a prophet, Anna the daughter of Phanuel, of the tribe of Asher. She was of a great age, having lived with her husband seven years after her marriage, (37) then as a widow to the age of eighty-four. She never left the temple but worshiped there with fasting and prayer night and day. (38) At that moment she came, and began to praise God and to speak about the child to all who were looking for the redemption of Jerusalem.

(39) When they had finished everything required by the law of the Lord, they returned to Galilee, to their own town of Nazareth. (40) The child grew and became strong, filled with wisdom; and the favor of God was upon him.

An elderly woman prophet named Anna is in the temple when the Holy Family arrives. This may be surprising since all the famous OT prophets (Isaiah, Jeremiah, Ezekiel) were men, but Israel did have women prophets. When king Josiah (640–609 BC) wanted to know the will of the Lord concerning a newly discovered book of the Law, he sent a distinguished delegation, led by the high priest, to consult a woman prophet named Huldah. She replied in classic prophetic language, "Thus says the LORD, the God of Israel," and answered the king's question. The delegation took the message back to the king who obeyed Huldah's words (2 Kgs 22:11-20).

Luke records no words of Anna but just says that she spoke "about the child to all who were looking for the redemption of Jerusalem" (2:38), the Holy City here symbolizing the Jewish people. Again Luke emphasizes the role of women.

With all the events of the infancy narrative having been concluded, the Holy Family returns "to their own town of Nazareth" (2:39).

PASTORAL REFLECTION

In this brief passage we see Luke at his best and worst. He notes the presence of a woman, but he puts no words in her mouth as he does for Simeon. Luke acknowledges the divine gift of prophecy to Anna, but he not show it in its fullness. In our communities, we will always find people of different gifts; indeed, we, too, have our own unique gifts. The community profits most when we accept those gifts and do so unconditionally as we can wish Luke had done here.

The Boy Jesus in the Temple (2:41-51)

(41) Now every year his parents went to Jerusalem for the festival of the Passover. (42) And when he was twelve years old, they went up as usual for the festival. (43) When the festival was ended and they started to return, the boy Jesus stayed behind in Jerusalem, but his parents did not know it. (44) Assuming that he was in the group of travelers, they went a day's journey. Then they started to look for him among their relatives and friends. (45) When they did not find him, they returned to Jerusalem to search for him. (46) After three days they

> *found him in the temple, sitting among the teachers, lis-*
> *tening to them and asking them questions. (47) And all*
> *who heard him were amazed at his understanding and*
> *his answers. (48) When his parents saw him, they were*
> *astonished; and his mother said to him, "Child, why*
> *have you treated us like this? Look, your father and I*
> *have been searching for you in great anxiety." (49) He*
> *said to them, "Why were you searching for me? Did you*
> *not know that I must be in my Father's house?" (50) But*
> *they did not understand what he said to them. (51) Then*
> *he went down with them and came to Nazareth, and*
> *was obedient to them. His mother treasured all these*
> *things in her heart.*

Luke closes his infancy narrative with the only account of Jesus between his birth and public ministry, namely, the family's trip to the temple in Jerusalem when he was twelve. Luke started his infancy narrative in the temple, and now he finishes it there.

The family visits the Holy City during Passover, the holiest time of the Jewish year. Presumably they piously fulfilled their religious duties and enjoyed the sights of the metropolis, but Luke says nothing about their stay in Jerusalem, focusing instead on their return. The parents leave without Jesus, and only after a day's travel do they realize that Jesus is not with their group. After a fruitless search among groups of friends and relatives, they return to Jerusalem. "After three days they found him in the temple, sitting among the teachers, listening to them and asking them questions. And all who heard him were amazed at his understanding and his answers" (2:46-47). This account hardly presents a flattering portrait of Mary and Joseph, who, we may safely presume, realized much sooner than Luke says that Jesus was missing. Probably Luke has a symbolic intent: they find him after three days, just as his disciples would encounter him after his three days in the tomb.

Verse 2:48 recalls verse 2:33, that is, Jesus' parents are astonished. Again, we wonder why, given all that has happened, and again scholars believe that this passage was once independent and integrated by Luke into his infancy narrative.

Since this will be Joseph's last appearance in the gospel, Luke pays him an often overlooked compliment. Jesus can answer the questions of the teachers so well that they are amazed. The religious training of a boy would have been the responsibility of his father, so here Luke shows us that Joseph has done a superb job in bringing up his son to be a good Jew. Even the temple scholars are impressed by this small town Galilean boy.

Jesus' words to his distraught parents can be disturbing to modern Christians: "Why were you searching for me? Did you not know that I must be in my Father's house?" (2:49). After all, a bright twelve-year-old would surely know why his parents were searching for him. But Luke has a theological intent. As the infancy narrative draws to a close, the evangelist shows Jesus for the first time withdrawing, however slightly, from his earthly parents, preparing the reader for his public ministry on behalf of his heavenly parent and for an expanded notion of his earthly family: "My mother and my brothers are those who hear the word of God and do it" (8:21). As always, the infancy narrative points us toward the remainder of the gospel.

The Holy Family returns to Nazareth, and "his mother treasured all these things in her heart" (2:51), paralleling her reaction to the account of the shepherds (2:19). Again Luke focuses on the woman, not the man.

PASTORAL REFLECTION

Whenever I heard this story as a boy, the teacher or preacher always assured the class or congregation that Joseph and Mary really were responsible parents, and since Jesus was divine—which, of course, they knew—he never was in any real danger (presumably he could miraculously fend off any danger). That approach may have been fine for children, but we would be better to see Mary and Joseph as normal parents in a difficult situation, which gives them relevance to us. Why should we not identify with their concern about a missing child? With their disappointment and frustration over their failure to check to make sure he was with relatives? With their anguished puzzlement about why they did not think about him sooner? Any parent can imagine their relief when they found him.

As I have indicated, Jesus was probably not missing for three full days and Luke here has a primarily theological intent, but I still believe that we can draw value from the narrative by relating to parents who made a mistake, as all parents do. The more humanly we view Joseph and Mary, the more we can understand them, and the better we understand them, the better we will understand their son.

And Jesus increased in wisdom and in years, and in divine and human favor (2:52).

CHAPTER FIVE

After the New Testament

No author can foresee, much less control, how a book will be received after it has been published. Some books become enormous commercial successes; others reach a limited but appreciative audience. Some books actually change how we view our world while others languish in obscurity.

In the 80s of the first century, two Greek-speaking Christians whom we call Matthew and Luke, one a Diasporan Jew, one a Gentile, both probably living in the Eastern Mediterranean provinces of the Roman Empire, wrote accounts of Jesus, their Lord, for the members of their local communities. The members of those communities already knew much about Jesus, thanks to the teaching of the apostle Paul and other, now anonymous, missionaries and preachers. They also probably knew about Jesus from a writing we call the Gospel of Mark, since the other two evangelists set out to deal, at least partially, with possible misunderstandings caused by that gospel.

Matthew wrote for a mixed community, but one with a sizeable, possibly even majority, Jewish element. Luke wrote, at least superficially, to give an orderly account about Jesus for his literary patron Theophilus, but really for a largely Gentile community. Like all writers, the evangelists wrote for their intended audiences, thus giving portraits of Jesus as he was understood by the writers and their communities.

Their approach mirrored that of their predecessor Mark and of their successors, John, author of the fourth canonical gospel, and other writers of gospels which the early church did not accept into the canon.

But Matthew and Luke enjoyed a success that the other gospel writers could not dream of. They included accounts of Jesus' birth, primarily to correct a possible misimpression from Mark's gospel that God's recognition of Jesus as his son was somehow connected or possibly even caused by his acceptance of baptism from the charismatic preacher and prophet John the Baptist. That the introductions to their gospels would become the best-known parts of their gospels and, indeed, of the entire New Testament, would have astonished not just Matthew and Luke but other early Christians as well, since no other biblical book gives any account of Jesus' birth. Why was this now celebrated event of so little importance?

The other NT writers did not, of course, say something like, "I did not discuss the birth of Jesus because . . . ," so scholars have to make learned estimates. We do know that the earliest Christians, including the apostle Paul (1 Thess 4:13-18; 1 Cor 15:51-58), expected to be alive when Jesus returned at the Second Coming. With history about to end, possibly they had little interest even in Jesus' own history.

But as time went on and the Second Coming did not occur, slowly Christians began to question an imminent end. In the Acts of the Apostles, Luke does not attack this idea, but he does weaken it by showing that the church is not just a group of people huddled together, waiting for the skies to open. Rather he presents the church as an instrument of God's continuing providential work not just among Christians but among the peoples of the world. As he did in the Old Testament, God continues to act in history.

This idea gradually sank in, and by the time of 2 Peter, the last NT book to be written, belief in an imminent end was fading fast. The author of 2 Peter (scholars do not believe that Peter of the twelve apostles wrote this letter) tries to shore up belief with the unconvincing argument that "with the Lord one day is like a thousand years, and a thousand years are like one day" (3:8), that is, the End is still near, but we just do not know how the Lord is calculating it. But this and other arguments (2 Pet 3:8-13) failed to move people, and by the mid-second century Christians had accepted Luke's belief that they would be in the world for some time to come, an attitude reflected in the passing of wandering prophets and speakers in tongues and in their replacement by less exotic but more reliable ministers like bishops, presbyters, and deacons.

Also by the mid-second century Christians had begun to argue that some of their books, and not just those of the Hebrew Bible, were inspired by God. This new notion took people aback, and it took a while to catch on. Around 200, one Egyptian theologian, Clement of Alexandria, first used the phrase "New Testament" to mean a collection of books, but his brilliant student, Origen, around 220 spoke of the "*so-called* New Testament."

But the idea of inspired Christian books gained ground in the second and third centuries, and we find a number of early Christian writers providing lists of titles that they considered to be inspired and which belonged in a canon or list of books. Right from the beginning, these canon lists included the four gospels of Matthew, Mark, Luke, and John, reflecting the growing interest in Jesus' earthly life. The inclusion of Matthew and Luke also guaranteed that the infancy narratives would always be read in the church.

The popularity of the infancy narratives appeared in another way. If imitation is indeed the sincerest form of flattery, then the gospels of Matthew and Luke were widely flattered in this era. By about 150 an anonymous Syrian Christian had written the *Protoevangelium of James*, a long account of Jesus' birth which also gives an account of the birth of Mary and the courtship between her and Joseph. It included elements not found in the canonical infancy narratives, such as the ox and the donkey (borrowed from Isa 1:3) as well as the names of Mary's parents, Joachim and Anna. Also from Syria and from the late second or early third century is the *Infancy Gospel of Thomas* which purports to tell of Jesus' childhood, strangely portraying him as an obnoxious brat who uses his miraculous powers as much to harm as to heal. For better or worse, these noncanonical or apocryphal gospels augmented the importance of Jesus' birth and thus of the canonical gospels that told of it.

Mainstream Christian writers began to cite the infancy narratives. Ignatius of Antioch (died ca. 117), a heroic bishop thrown to the lions in the Roman circus, spoke about the star followed by the magi, proclaiming that it was so bright that it outshone all the other stars (now a staple of Christmas cards). Ignatius also speculated on the homeland of the magi. A late second-century writer, Irenaeus of Lyons (died ca. 180), provided a symbolic interpretation of the gifts of the magi. By 200, Origen of Alexandria claimed that there were three magi; he did not explain why he said this, but it is probably because there were three gifts. Early Christian speculation about the infancy narratives continued well into the sixth century when the magi had acquired royal stature and names, Jesus had acquired a birth date (December 25), and sermons on the Nativity abounded.

The biggest change in understanding the infancy narratives occurred in the fourth century when the church instituted a feast to commemorate Jesus' birth. Called in Latin the *dies natalis Christi*, the "natal [= birth] day of Christ," this feast traveled with the Christian missionaries into northern and western Europe, including a country called England where in the eleventh century people began calling it "Christmas," derived from the phrase "Christ's mass," a reference to midnight mass which ended the fasting season of Advent.

Christmas has, of course, become the lens through which we view the birth of Jesus. I love Christmas, and my love for the feast and the season accompanying it includes many of the legends and traditions. A student once asked me if I have two Christmas crèches, one for Luke and one for Matthew. After the laughter stopped, I assured him that the answer was no, that my crèche included the ox and the donkey and the three kings and their camels, and that even scholars can enjoy a traditional Christmas.

There may be a big difference between enjoying a traditional Christmas and understanding the Scriptures, but a difference does not mean a conflict. We can celebrate Christmas with all the tradition we want, but we cannot be responsible Christians if we ignore the Scriptures. Matthew and Luke did not write for a nonexistent feast day. They wrote in the first century for their own communities, and that is how we must approach their infancy narratives. If we use this approach, we can understand the infancy narratives, appreciate and enjoy the remarkable feast that has grown up about them, and get an insight into the Scriptures, God's ever-giving gift to his people.

Suggested Reading

The translation of the Bible used in preparing this work was the New Revised Standard Version (NRSV). Sometimes I also referred to other well-known terms associated with the infancy narratives, such as "magi" and "swaddling clothes," although the NRSV translates them differently.

The infancy narratives are introductions of two gospels, so every commentary on Matthew and Luke discusses them. Since this book is for the general reader, I will not list a series of scholarly commentaries but instead recommend the *New Collegeville Bible Commentary* New Testament Series, published by Liturgical Press. The series is available in twelve individual volumes (one each for Matthew and Luke). The original New Testament volumes are included in the one-volume Old and New Testament commentary, edited by Dianne Bergant. Although such a large commentary may seem like too much for your needs, you will find that information on Old Testament books, especially Isaiah, will be helpful in understanding the infancy narratives, and that information on the other New Testament books will fill in some gaps. Also, as you learn more about the infancy narratives, you may find that you would like to learn more about the Bible in general. And, of course, you can look up the infancy narratives in the commentaries on the gospels of Matthew and Luke.

Another valuable one-volume commentary for the general reader is *Harper's Bible Commentary*, revised edition (San Francisco: Harper & Row, 2000), edited by James Mays, an ecumenical volume with contributors from many different traditions.

The classic study of the infancy narratives is by Raymond E. Brown, *The Birth of the Messiah* (New York: Doubleday, second edition, 1993). This massive work contains the most detailed study of the infancy narratives ever made. The nonspecialist reader may not find it useful, but all of us writing about the infancy narratives are in Father Brown's debt, and all those interested in this topic must know of this book.

A good introduction to the infancy narratives for the general reader is *The Drama of Christ's Coming* by Wilfrid Harrington (Wilmington, DE: Michael Glazier Books, 1986). It is clear and filled with good insights.

Much of Matthew's infancy narrative cites fulfillment of OT prophecies; for a good modern treatment of that issue, try *No Trace of Christmas? Discovering Advent in the Old Testament* by Christoph Dolmen (Collegeville, MN: Liturgical Press, 2000).

The infancy narratives, especially Luke, say much about Mary. Still valuable is an ecumenical study entitled *Mary in the New Testament*, edited by Raymond E. Brown and Karl Donfried (Philadelphia: Fortress Press, 1978, and Mahwah, NJ: Paulist Press, 1978). Elizabeth Johnson's *Truly Our Sister: A Theology of Mary in the Communion of Saints* (New York: Continuum, 2003) has an excellent account of modern scriptural approaches to Mary.

To get a good sense of how the Synoptic Gospels both parallel and differ from one another, consult *Gospel Parallels*, edited by Burton Throckmorton (Toronto: Thomas Nelson, 1992). When you look up an individual episode, such as the disciples' picking grain on the Sabbath, you can clearly see how Matthew, Mark, and Luke covered the same topic but with their own emphases and insights.

Was there a celestial phenomenon at Jesus' birth? Two modern astronomers have examined the question: Mark Kidger, *The Star of Bethlehem: An Astronomer's View* (Princeton, NJ: Princeton University Press, 1999), and Michael Molnar, *The Star of Bethlehem: The Legacy of the Magi* (New Brunswick, NJ: Rutgers University Press, 2000), and they conclude the answer is yes.

The book of Isaiah had a significant impact on how generations of Christians understood the NT, especially the infancy narratives and Jesus' mother Mary. A fine and readable study of this impact is *The Fifth Gospel: Isaiah in the History of Christianity* by John Sawyer (Cambridge: Cambridge University Press, 1996).

A good general introduction to the New Testament is *The New Testament: A Historical Introduction to the Early Christian Writings*, second edition, by Bart Ehrman (New York: Oxford University Press, 2000). Catholic readers may find helpful my *An Introduction to the New Testament for Catholics* (Collegeville, MN: Liturgical Press, 2006). *The Cambridge Companion to the Bible* by Howard Clark Kee, Eric Meyers, John Rogerson, and Anthony Saldarini (New York: Cambridge University Press, 1997) provides an introduction to the entire Bible with useful sidebars explaining difficult terms or historical questions along with many photographs. These texts will point the reader to other, more specialized works.

An excellent reference work is *Dictionary of New Testament Background*, edited by Craig Stevens and Stanley Porter (Downers Grove, IL: InterVarsity Press, 2000). This offers detailed articles on all the major topics necessary to understand more about the world in which the NT and thus the infancy narratives arose. For example, the Holy Family went to the temple in Jerusalem, and this book offers a detailed but readable account of what the temple was and what it meant to the ancient Jews.

There are many apocryphal accounts of Jesus' birth. A good collection of them is *The Apocryphal Jesus*, edited by J. K. Elliott (New York: Oxford University Press, 1996).

If you wish to know how the now familiar traditions about the birth of Jesus grew up (the three kings, the ox and the donkey at the crib, the date of December 25), my book *The Origins of Christmas* (Collegeville, MN: Liturgical Press, 2004) explains all of those.

This book stresses that the infancy narratives should be understood as the introductory chapters to the gospels of Matthew and Luke. The best way to understand these narratives is to read the entire gospels and, in Luke's case, to read the Acts of the Apostles as well. As you understand the gospels better, you will see how the infancy narratives fit into them. But, as we have seen, even these four brief gospel chapters presume so much else—a knowledge of some of the prophets, Jewish customs, earlier Christian literature (Paul's epistles, the Gospel of Mark)—so let me express my hope that this brief book may encourage you to get to know much more of the Bible in its entirety.